The Book of Daniel
"The Most High Rules"

Lucian Farrar, Jr.

James Kay Publishing

Tulsa, Oklahoma

The Book of Daniel
"The Most High Rules"
ISBN 978-0-9850113-9-0

www.jameskaypublishing.com

e-mail: sales@jameskaypublishing.com

© 2014 Lucian Farrar, Jr.
Cover design by JKP
Author Photo by Bob Cooper

also by
Lucian Farrar, Jr.

The Victorious Church
In the Book of Revelation
A Commentary and Questions

The Minor Prophets
God's Spokesmen
A Commentary and Questions

The Book of Isaiah
Christ, Our Redeemer
A Commentary and Questions

The Life of Christ
A Chronological Account

Psalms
Book 1
David's Original Collection

Psalms
Books 2 & 3

Scriptures are from the King James Version with archaic words, forms, and punctuations replaced by those in current use.

Other translations are acknowledged by the following abbreviations:
ASV – American Standard Version
ESV – English Standard Version
NASB – New American Standard Bible
NIV – New International Version
NKJV – New King James Version

Dedication

To my wife, LuEllen, who has been by my side with help and encouragement for over fifty years. She has given us four wonderful children, who love and serve the Lord. By her example, she has shown me the importance of being kind, thoughtful, and generous. When I hear her singing, she lifts my spirit with her beautiful alto voice. Her life is a demonstration of one who is living by faith in God.

— Lucian Farrar, Jr.
2014

Table of Contents

Lesson 1

The Book of Daniel
"The Most High Rules"

Daniel was just a teenager when he was taken to Babylon to be trained for service in the government of the Babylonian Empire. In the opening chapters he writes about the experiences that he and his three friends had as young Jews in a foreign land. Their faithfulness to God caused the proud king Nebuchadnezzar to acknowledge the LORD as *"the King of heaven . . . whose works are truth."* [4:37] God gave Daniel the ability to interpret the king's dreams and predict future events. Daniel was over 80 years old when he interpreted the handwriting on the wall, the night Babylon fell to the Medes and Persians. He was so well respected that he was made a high official in the new government of King Darius the Mede. When the LORD delivered Daniel from the lions, this new king sent a decree to all the nations that dwell on the earth that they must *"tremble and fear before the God of Daniel, for he is the living God."* [6:26] From youth to old age, Daniel faithfully obeyed the LORD while serving in two great world empires. The book of Daniel spans 72 years from 606 to 534 BC.

The Theme

"The Most High rules in the kingdom of men." [4:17] This is the theme of the book of Daniel and the history of the world. *"He removes kings, and he sets up kings."* [2:21]

The Historical Setting

God judged the wicked world in the days of Noah by destroying it with a flood, but he saved righteous Noah and his family and gave the human race a new beginning.

The Lord blessed Abraham, Isaac, and Jacob as his chosen family, while promising, *"In your seed shall all the nations of the earth be blessed."* Through his providence, God elevated Joseph from a slave to a ruler in Egypt so he could save his people. Later, his family was forced to serve the Egyptians. With ten plagues, God demonstrated his great power over Pharaoh. He delivered his people from their bondage by destroying the Egyptian army in the Red Sea.[1]

God revealed himself at Mount Sinai when he made his covenant with the nation of Israel and Moses. With God's power, Joshua conquered the wicked inhabitants of Canaan and established the nation of Israel in the land of promise.[2]

When the elders of Israel asked for a king, the LORD said, *"They have rejected me that I should not reign over them."* [1 Samuel 8:7] Although Saul was made king of Israel, the prophet Samuel warned the nation, *"But if you will not obey the voice of the LORD, but rebel against the commandment of the LORD, then shall the hand of the LORD be against you."* [1 Samuel 12:15] God established the throne of David, who conquered all his enemies and made Jerusalem the capital city. When his son Solomon became king, God blessed him with wisdom, riches and honor. At the dedication of the beautiful temple in Jerusalem, Solomon asked God to *"hear from heaven, your dwelling place. Forgive and*

---

[1] Genesis 22:18; Genesis 45:4-5; Exodus 1:1 – 15:21
[2] Exodus 19:1 – 34:28; Joshua 1:1-9; Joshua 23:1 – 24:31

act; deal with each man according to all he does, since you know his heart." [1 Kings 8:39, NIV]

But Solomon married many foreign women, and when he was old, his wives turned his heart after other gods. Because of his sins, the kingdom of Israel was divided. The LORD gave Jeroboam the kingdom of Israel and left Solomon's son Rehoboam with only two tribes in the kingdom of Judah.[3]

God promised to build for Jeroboam an enduring dynasty as he had done for David if he would obey him. However, Jeroboam rebelled against the LORD by erecting golden calves for the people to worship at Bethel and at Dan. His son Nadab was killed after reigning only two years over Israel, and Jeroboam's dynasty came to an end. The remaining kings of Israel were also guilty of *"the sins of Jeroboam."* Kings from nine separate families reigned over the northern kingdom of Israel, while God continued to place a descendant of David on the throne in Jerusalem over the southern kingdom of Judah.[4] Because of idolatry and other sins, the kingdom of Israel fell in 722 BC to the Assyrians. The LORD had predicted the destruction of Israel when they were enjoying peace and great prosperity.

The kingdom of Judah survived the invasion of the Assyrians and continued for another 136 years after the fall of Israel. Jerusalem was protected because King Hezekiah put his trust in the LORD, who then killed 185,000 of the army that was besieging the city.[5]

The prophet Isaiah had predicted the fall of Babylon to the Medes and Persians before any of these nations

---

[3] 1 Kings 11:1-37
[4] 1 Kings 11:37-38 cf. 2 Samuel 7:12; 1 Kings 12:26-29; 1 Kings 16:31; 2 Kings 10:29; 2 Kings 15:18, 24, 28
[5] 1 Kings 18:13 – 19:37

came to power.[6] He called Cyrus by name at least 150 years before he became the king of Persia.[7]

In 612 BC the Assyrian Empire came to an end with the destruction of the city of Nineveh, as predicted by Nahum, the prophet of the LORD. Babylon became the next great empire under the Chaldean king Nebuchadnezzar.

The Time of Daniel

Daniel was living at this time. Josiah, the last good king of Judah, had repaired the temple in Jerusalem and restored the worship of the LORD.[8] Daniel must have grown up admiring this godly man who became king at an early age. Josiah was a devout and humble servant of God. He knew God was bringing calamity upon Jerusalem and the kingdom of Judah because of the sins of his father and grandfather.[9] As a young boy living in Jerusalem, Daniel heard the prophet Jeremiah preaching, *"Thus says the LORD 'Stand ye in the ways and see, and ask for the old paths, where is the good way, and walk therein.'"* [Jeremiah 6:16]

No doubt Daniel was greatly disturbed when Josiah was killed in a battle against Egypt. Jehoiakim, a wicked son of Josiah, was made the next king of Judah.[10] The LORD comforted his prophet Habakkuk, who also was troubled by these conditions. His words of encouragement were, *"The just shall live by his faith."* [Habakkuk 2:4] This message would sustain Daniel for the rest of his life. In the book of Daniel we see the just living by faith in the Most High, who rules the kingdom of men.

---

[6] Isaiah 13; Isaiah 21:1-9
[7] Isaiah 44:28 – 45:7
[8] 2 Kings 22:1 – 23:27
[9] 2 Kings 21:1-24; 2 Kings 22:26-27
[10] 2 Kings 23:28-37

In 606 BC, Daniel was among the first captives of Judah to be deported to Babylon. The second deportation came in 597 BC, when the prophet Ezekiel was taken to Babylon along with 10,000 other Jews. The temple and the city of Jerusalem were destroyed in 586 BC, and the third group of captives was taken to Babylon.

Daniel's Authorship Questioned

Some Bible scholars contend that Daniel could not have written the book that bears his name because it accurately predicts events that were hundreds of years after he lived. F. W. Farrar states that Daniel was written "by a holy and gifted Jew" after 165 BC. [11] However, the writer identifies himself with the words, *"I, Daniel,"* and claims to be a man living in the time of Belshazzar king of Babylon and during the reigns of Darius the Mede and Cyrus of Persia.[12] If the book of Daniel was written by a Jew in the second century, he may have been "gifted," but he could not have been "holy." He would have been a liar! As Stafford North concluded, "The Book of Daniel cannot be the work of an honest, well-meaning forger. Either it is an amazing prophecy or it is a fraud. The book was written **when** and **where** it claims and does speak accurately of events several hundred years in the future." [13]

The amazing prophecies of Daniel do not end with the defeat of Antiochus IV in 165 BC. In chapter 7, Daniel writes about the Roman Empire that would be preceded by the Babylonians, the Medes and Persians, and the Greeks. Daniel correctly predicted that the eleventh Roman king *"shall speak pompous words against the*

---

[11] F. W. Farrar, *The Book of Daniel*, p. 119
[12] Daniel 8:1; Daniel 9:1-2; Daniel 10:1-2
[13] Stafford North, *Studies in Daniel*, p. 6

Most High" and *"shall persecute the saints of the Most High."* [7:25, NKJV] This is a very accurate description of Domitian, who reigned over the Roman Empire from AD 81 to 96 and was known for his persecution of Christians.[14] How would "a gifted Jew" in the second century BC know about Domitian and the Roman Empire? The argument against Daniel's authorship could be used against a Jewish author in 165 BC.

The liberal critics argue that the book of Daniel is not prophetic, because the Hebrew Bible does not include it in the section of "The Prophets" but in the section called "The Writings." This is a weak argument for three reasons. (1) The Hebrew Bible has Daniel just before Ezra and Nehemiah. This is a logical placement because Daniel reports historical events during the exile in Babylon just before the books that relate the return from the exile. (2) The Holy Spirit calls David "a prophet" in Acts 2:30, and in the Hebrew Bible his Psalms are in "The Writings" along with Daniel. The New Testament uses prophecies in the Psalms to prove that Jesus is the Christ.[15] (3) As a prophet, Moses was a type of Christ.[16] His prophecies are no less prophetic because they are in "The Law" section instead of being with "The Prophets" in the Hebrew Bible. Although Moses was known as a lawgiver and David as a king and Daniel as a statesman, all three of them were prophets as well. These critics may be described in the words of Romans 1:22, *"Professing themselves to be wise, they became fools."*

The book of Daniel was written by Daniel, an exiled Jew who was an official in both the Babylonian and Persian governments from his teenage years to his death at an old age.

---

[14] Paul L. Maier, *Eusebius—The Church History*, p. 107
[15] John 19:24, 36; Acts 2:25-35; Acts 13:33-35; Hebrews 2:6-12; Hebrews 7:17, 21
[16] Deuteronomy 18:15-19; Acts 3:18-23; Acts 7:37, 52

Ezekiel, a contemporary, testifies that Daniel was well known for his righteousness and wisdom during the time of the exile.[17] He is mentioned along with Noah and Job as a real person, not a fictional character.

Josephus, the Jewish historian in the first century, reports that Alexander the Great was shown the prophecy of Daniel 8:5-21 when he came to Jerusalem in 332 BC, and he understood that he was fulfilling it.[18]

Mattathias, the father of Judas Maccabeus, encouraged the revolt in 168 BC against Antiochus IV by reminding his people that "Daniel…was delivered from the mouth of lions." [1 Maccabees 2:60]

Jesus recognized Daniel as a historical person and called him *"the prophet"* in Matthew 24:15. He referred to Daniel's prophecy concerning the destruction of Jerusalem that was to be fulfilled in the first century.[19] His testimony should remove all doubts about the authenticity of the book of Daniel.

The Purpose of the Book of Daniel

Daniel is encouraging his people to be faithful to the LORD. Even though a descendant of David is no longer on a throne in Jerusalem, God is still on his throne in heaven. Although the temple of the Lord in Jerusalem is destroyed, *"The LORD is in his holy temple* (in heaven). *Let all the earth keep silence before him."* With the city of Jerusalem in ashes, *"the earth shall be filled with the knowledge of the glory of the LORD."* Daniel is showing that God is fulfilling the promises he made to the

---

[17] Ezekiel 14:14, 20 and Ezekiel 28:3
[18] Flavius Josephus, *Antiquities*, XI, viii, 5
[19] Daniel 9:27; Matthew 24:15, 34

prophet Habakkuk.[20] During the exile in Babylon, *"the just shall live by his faith."* God will keep his promise, and the Jews will be allowed to return to Jerusalem after seventy years in Babylon.[21] In the distant future from Daniel's time of writing, the Jews will be severely persecuted, but God will deliver them. In the days of the fourth kingdom, the Roman Empire, the God of heaven will set up a kingdom that will never be destroyed.[22]

The Structure of the Book of Daniel

The book of Daniel is divided into two equal parts. The first six chapters are about the life of Daniel. In this section, we can see God working in history. As he rules the kingdom of men, the Most High provides, reveals, protects, humbles, judges, and delivers. The last six chapters are prophetic visions that Daniel saw during the time of the events covered in the first six chapters.

---

[20] Habakkuk 2:20, Habakkuk 2:14, Habakkuk 2:4
[21] Jeremiah 29:10
[22] Daniel 2:44; Daniel 7:13-14

An Outline of Daniel

I. The Life of Daniel, Chapters 1-6
Chapter 1 – God **Provides** for the Pure in Heart
Chapter 2 – God **Reveals** Future Kingdoms
Chapter 3 – God **Protects** the Faithful from Fire
Chapter 4 – God **Humbles** a Proud King
Chapter 5 – God **Judges** the Kingdom of Babylon
Chapter 6 – God **Delivers** Daniel from the Lions

II. The Prophecies of Daniel, Chapters 7-12
Chapter 7 – The Four Beasts
Chapter 8 – The Ram and the Goat
Chapter 9 – The Seventy Weeks
Chapters 10-12 – The Latter Days of the Jews

Review Questions on Lesson 1

1. What is the theme of the book of Daniel? _____

2. The book of Daniel spans ____ years from _____ to _____ BC.

3. Daniel grew up during the reign of King _____.

4. When Daniel was a boy, the prophet _____ was saying, "Ask for the old paths..."

5. Habakkuk the prophet was encouraged with these words: "The _____ shall live by his _____."

6. Daniel was among the first to be deported to Babylon in _____ BC.

7. The prophet _____ was part of the second deportation in 597 BC.

8. The third deportation and the destruction of Jerusalem and the temple was in the year _____ BC.

9. Why do some liberal critics reject Daniel's authorship of the book?_____

10. The writer says that he is _____ and he is living in the time of _____ king of Babylon and during the reigns of king _____ the Mede and _____ king of Persia. [Daniel 8:1, 9:1-2, 10:1-2]

11. The seventh chapter of Daniel very accurately describes _____, the eleventh Roman king, who lived over 200 years after the time that the critics say the book was written.

12. Why is Daniel before Ezra and Nehemiah in the Hebrew Bible? _____
_____
_____

13. Like Daniel, both _____ and _____ were prophets whose writings are not in the section of "The Prophets" in the Hebrew Bible.

14. As a contemporary of Daniel, _____ testifies of Daniel's righteousness and wisdom.

15. Jesus called Daniel, "the _____." [Matt. 24:15]

16. What was Daniel's purpose in writing the book?
_____
_____

17. Daniel shows that God is fulfilling his promise that "the earth shall be filled with the _____ of the _____ of the Lord." [Habakkuk 2:14]

18. God is keeping his promise that after _____ years in Babylon, the Jews will be able to return to Jerusalem.

19. In the distant future from Daniel's time, the Jews would be _____, but God would deliver them.

20. The God of heaven shall set up a _____ that shall never be destroyed. [Daniel 2:44]

21. The first six chapters are about the _____ of Daniel.

22. The last six chapters are about the _____ of Daniel

23. What six things does God do, according to the first six chapters of Daniel? _____, _____,
_____, _____, _____.
and _____.(See the outline of the book.)

NOTES

Lesson 2

God Provides for the Pure in Heart

Daniel 1

The Lord Gave Jerusalem to Nebuchadnezzar

Daniel 1:1-2

In 609 BC, Josiah king of Judah was killed in battle at Megiddo by the Egyptian army. Pharaoh Necho placed Josiah's son Jehoiakim on the throne of Judah. King Jehoiakim led the people back into idolatry. He persecuted the prophet Jeremiah and burned the scroll on which the prophet had written words of warning from the LORD. [2 Kings 23:29-37; Jeremiah 36:1-23]

Nebuchadnezzar's Babylonian army came up against the city of Jerusalem in 606 BC, and *the Lord gave Jehoiakim king of Judah into his hand.* 1:1-2 The theme of Daniel can be seen in these opening verses: "The Most High rules in the kingdom of men." [4:17]

Nebuchadnezzar did not become the king of Babylon until 605 BC, a year later. His being called "king of Babylon" in verse one is a **prolepsis**, "the representation or assumption of a future act or development as if presently existing or accomplished." [23] Acts 7:2 is an example of a prolepsis. Stephen said, *"The God of glory appeared to our father Abraham when he was in Mesopotamia, before he dwelt in Haran,"* and then he quoted Genesis 12:1. But in this verse, God is speaking to *Abram.* His name was changed to *Abraham* many years later in Genesis 17:5. Similarly, Nebuchadnezzar was not king when he first came up against Jerusalem, but he was king when Daniel wrote about it. This is not an error as charged by some critics.

---

[23] *Webster's Ninth New Collegiate Dictionary*

Nebuchadnezzar carried some of the vessels from the temple of God into the land of Shinar. **1:2** The ancient Hebrew name for Babylon was "Shinar" as seen in Genesis 10:10 and 11:2. Daniel's use of this name is proof that he is the writer in the sixth century BC, because the name was no longer used in the second century BC.[24] Later, these vessels from the temple were profaned by Belshazzar in Daniel 5.

Daniel's Training in Babylon, 1:3-7

Ashpenaz, the chief of Nebuchadnezzar's court officials, brought Daniel and other young men from Jerusalem to Babylon to be trained for three years in order to enter the king's service. **1:3, 5** Daniel was in Babylon and Persia for at least 72 years, from 606 BC to 534 BC. This means that he was probably a teenager when he was taken away from his home. Daniel and the others were of the royal family and of the nobles of Judah. This fulfilled Isaiah's prophecy made to Hezekiah king of Judah, when he said to him, *"And of your sons that shall issue from you, which you shall beget ... they shall take away, and they shall be eunuchs in the palace of the king of Babylon."* [Isaiah 39:7]

Daniel and the other young Jews had no physical defect; they were handsome, intelligent, teachable, and quick to understand. They were to be taught the language and the literature of the Babylonians. **1:4** Their educations included courses in the Babylonian culture. Like Joseph and Moses, Daniel did not lose his faith in God by being exposed to heathen science and myths. He rejected those things that did not agree with God's revealed truth.

---

[24] Burton Coffman, *Coffman's Bible Commentary*, Daniel 1:2

New names were given to Daniel and his three friends. **1:6, 7** The name *Daniel* means "God is my judge," but the Babylonians gave him the new name *Belteshazzar* meaning "Bel protects." His three associates had Hebrew names that gave glory to God — *Hananiah, Mishael, and Azariah.* But their new Babylonian names — *Shadrack, Meshach,* and *Abed-Nego* — honored pagan gods. These names were something that had to be endured. They knew who they were. They would glorify God by their lives regardless of the names they were called. The Bible instructs us to *"glorify God in your body and in your spirit, which are God's."* [1 Corinthians 6:20]

Daniel Purposed to be Pure in Heart, 1:8-16

As part of their training, the young men were to be fed the best food from the king's table. [1:5] However, the meats and the wine had been sacrificed to idols, and partaking of them would be considered as worshiping their gods. No doubt some of the royal food included meats that were unclean to the Jews. [1 Cor. 10:19-20; Leviticus 11]

"Daniel purposed in his heart that he would not defile himself with the portion of the king's meat, nor with the wine which he drank." **1:8** In God's providence, Daniel had been shown kindness by the chief official in charge of his training. **1:9** It's hard to say "No" to someone who has befriended you. This official was even afraid he would be put to death if Daniel was not well fed. **1:10**

It takes purpose to serve the Lord. Without it, we can drift into sin and error. Barnabas encouraged the Christians at Antioch to be faithful to the Lord *"with purpose of heart"*. [Acts 11:23] Although Daniel was just a teenager away from home, he did not believe "When in Babylon, do as the Babylonians do." He was obeying Proverbs 4:23, *"Keep your heart with all diligence; for out of it are the issues of life."* Later, Jesus promised, *"Blessed are the pure in heart: for they shall see God."* [Matthew 5:8]

Daniel spoke to the steward whom Ashpenaz had appointed over Daniel and his three friends. He proposed a ten-day test. For ten days Daniel, Hananiah, Mishael, and Azariah would eat only vegetables and drink only water. The steward agreed. *"And at the end of ten days their countenances appeared fairer and fatter . . . than all the children which did eat the portion of the king's meat."* 1:15

God Provided for Daniel, 1:17-21

God gave them knowledge and skill in all learning and wisdom: and Daniel had understanding in all visions and dreams. **1:17** At the end of their days of training, the eunuchs were brought before the king; *and among them all was found none like Daniel, Hananiah, Mishael, and Azariah. 1:18-19* They were the top of the class. In fact, the king had found their wisdom and understanding *ten times better than all the magicians and astrologers who were in all his realm.* The *"ten times"* may be a **hyperbole**, but the next chapter, Daniel 2, explains why such a statement was made. Daniel with the help of his three friends was able to do something that all of the wise men of Babylon were unable to do. He revealed the king's dream and interpreted its meaning. God provided for the pure in heart.

Daniel continued even unto the first year of king Cyrus. **1:21** Daniel writes about himself both in the third and first persons. [10:1-3] He lived to witness the decree by Cyrus that allowed the Jews to return to their homeland after his seventy years in Babylon. He outlived the Babylonians and became an officer in the Medo-Persian kingdom. [6:1-3]

In this first chapter, we can see God working in a providential way. He gave Jehoiakim and Jerusalem into Nebuchadnezzar's hand. He brought Daniel into the favor of Ashpenaz. He gave these four young men knowledge and skills. God allowed Daniel to see the fulfillment of Jeremiah's prophecy. [Jer. 29:10; Daniel 9:9]

Review Questions on Lesson 2

1. What is the outline heading for Daniel, chapter one?
   _____

2. What **prolepsis** (figure of speech) is used in Daniel 1:1?
   _____
   _____

3. Who gave Jehoiakim into Nebuchadnezzar's hand?
   _____

4. What did Nebuchadnezzar take to *Shinar* to his god?
   _____
   _____

5. What does the use of the word *Shinar* prove?
   _____
   _____

6. Who was Ashpenaz? _____

7. Daniel was trained for _____ years in Babylon.

8. Daniel was either of the _____ family or of the _____.

9. How did Daniel look? _____

10. What is said about Daniel's intelligence? _____
    _____

11. Ashpenaz gave new names to Daniel & his three friends:
    Daniel was named _____
    Hananiah was named _____
    Mishael was named _____
    Azariah was named _____

12. What did Daniel purpose in his heart? _____
    _____

13. What did Ashpenaz fear? _____

_____

14. How long was Daniel and his friends tested with a diet of vegetables and water? _____

15. What were the results? _____

_____

16. Who gave Daniel understanding? _____

17. How did Daniel and his three friends compare with all the wise men of Babylon? 1:20 _____

_____

18. What is significant about Daniel continuing until the first year of King Cyrus? _____

_____

_____

Important Dates

Three Deportations: Daniel in 606 BC
Ezekiel in 597 BC
The Third in 586 BC

Three Returns: First led by Zerubbabel in 536 BC
Second led by Ezra in 458 BC
Third led by Nehemiah in 445 BC

Other Key Dates: The Fall of Babylon in 539 BC
The Temple rebuilt in 516 BC
Esther made queen in 478 BC

[Dates from Stafford North, *Studies in Daniel,* pp. 53, 54]

Lesson 3

God Reveals Future Kingdoms
Daniel 2

Nebuchadnezzar's Dream
Daniel 2:1-13

Nebuchadnezzar was greatly troubled by a dream during the second year of his reign. **2:1** He became king one year after Daniel was taken to Babylon. Thus, Daniel was in his third year in Babylon and his last year of training. [1:5]

The king summoned his wise men to interpret the meaning of his dream. **2:2** When they asked what he had dreamed, he refused to tell them. Nebuchadnezzar said, *"Tell me the dream, and I shall know that you can show me the interpretation thereof."* **2:9** If they had the gifts of insight and psychic powers that they claimed to possess as magicians, astrologers, and sorcerers, they should have been able to tell the king his dream. However, they confessed that no one on earth could do it. They complained that no king or ruler had ever demanded such knowledge from his advisors and wise men. They concluded that no man could tell the king's dream; one would have to be a god, not a man, to do such a thing. **2:10, 11**

For this cause the king was angry and very furious. **2:12** Nebuchadnezzar ordered the execution of all the wise men of Babylon. Daniel and his companions were in this group that the king was seeking to kill. **2:13**

Daniel Seeks God's Help
Daniel 2:14-23

Daniel spoke with wisdom to Arioch, the captain of the king's guard, who was executing the wise men. He asked, *"Why is the decree so hasty from the king?"* **2:14, 15** Arioch informed Daniel of the events that led to the decree being made. Daniel then asked that he be given a "time" or an appointment to meet with the king to tell him the interpretation of the dream. This was an act of faith!

When he returned to his house, Daniel urged Hananiah, Mishael, and Azariah to pray for mercies concerning this secret. *Then was the secret revealed unto Daniel in a night vision.* **2:17-19** Daniel praised the God of heaven, who *"removes kings and sets up kings"* **2:21** and *"reveals the deep and secret things."* **2:22** Ezekiel made reference to God's revealing "secrets" to Daniel in Ezekiel 28:3.

Daniel Tells Nebuchadnezzar about God
Daniel 2:24-30

The next morning, Daniel asked Arioch to take him to the king, and he would tell him the interpretation of his dream. Arioch introduced Daniel as "a man of the captives of Judah." The king asked Daniel if he was able to tell him the dream and its interpretation. Daniel did not take credit for himself, but he said, *"There is a God in heaven that reveals secrets."* **2:28** Then Daniel explained the purpose of the dream. God is making known to king Nebuchadnezzar *what shall be in the latter days.* **2:28** He is speaking of the history of the

Jews, from the destruction of Jerusalem in 586 BC to its destruction again in AD 70. These were the last days of God's providential protection of the Jewish nation. The LORD had promised Habakkuk, *"The earth shall be filled with the knowledge of the glory of the LORD."* [Hab. 2:14]

God even revealed to Daniel the thoughts that the king had on his bed that prompted his dream. He was thinking about what would be in the future. Therefore, God made these things known to Daniel so that Nebuchadnezzar would know that the true God reveals secrets and makes known what shall come to pass. **2:29**

God Reveals the Dream and its Interpretation
Daniel 2:31-45

"You looked, O king, and there before you stood a large statue—an enormous, dazzling statue, awesome in appearance. The head of the statue was made of pure gold, its chest and arms of silver, its belly and thighs of bronze, its legs of iron, its feet partly of iron and partly of baked clay. While you were watching, a rock was cut out, but not by human hands. It struck the image on its feet of iron and clay and smashed them. Then the iron, the clay, the bronze, the silver and the gold were broken to pieces at the same time and became like chaff on a threshing floor in the summer. The wind swept them away without leaving a trace. But the rock that struck the statue became a huge mountain and filled the whole earth. This is the dream; and we will tell the interpretation." ᴺᴵⱽ **2:31-36** Daniel informs the king that he is not doing this by himself. God is telling him its meaning.

The *head of gold* represents Nebuchadnezzar and his Babylonian kingdom. The God of heaven had given him a kingdom, power, strength and glory. **2:37, 38** *"The Most High rules in the kingdom of men."* [4:17]

The *chest and arms of silver* represent a second kingdom that would replace the Babylonians. **2:39** According to Daniel 5:28 this kingdom would be the Medes and Persians.

The *belly and thighs of bronze* represent the third kingdom that would rule over all the earth. After the Medes and Persians would be the kingdom of Greece with Alexander the Great as its first king. [8:20-21]

The *legs of iron and feet of iron and clay* represent a fourth kingdom that would be strong like iron. **2:40** The Roman Empire followed the Greeks and was known for its powerful strength as it crushed all the other nations. The weakness that would be within the strong Roman Empire is represented by the feet of iron and clay. The LORD predicted that *the people will be a mixture and will not remain united, any more than iron mixes with clay.* **2:42-43** ᴺᴵⱽ The Roman Empire was a mixture of various peoples with diverse cultures; this division was one of the main reasons for its eventual fall. The Romans began with a strong republic (*legs of iron*), but it grew into an empire (*feet of iron and clay*). The kingdom was gradually weakened by the differences of the people under its power.

Although the toes are mentioned, they are not numbered. **2:41, 42** In the time of David, there was a giant of Gath who had twelve toes.[1 Chronicles 20:6] To say that the image had "ten toes" (as dispensational premillennialists do) is assuming something that the Bible does not tell us. If the number of toes were significant and prophetic, the number would have been given just as the *"two horns"* of the ram in Daniel 8:3. Normal rams have two horns, don't they? Also, their meaning would have been explained as in Daniel 8:20. The number is given because the *"two horns are the kings of Media and Persia."* If the toes are ten modern nations, the number would have been stated and the explanation made.

The LORD used the image in Nebuchadnezzar's dream to reveal the four kingdoms (the Babylonians, the Medes & Persians, the Greeks, and the Romans) that would precede the coming of God's eternal kingdom.

And in the days of these kings shall the God of heaven set up a kingdom, which shall never be destroyed. **2:44** Jesus was given *"the throne of David ... and of his kingdom there shall be no end."* [Luke 1:31-33] The birth and ministry of Jesus was in the time of the Roman kings, just as Daniel predicted. [Luke 2:1; 3:1] Jesus preached, *"The time is fulfilled, and the kingdom of God is at hand."* [Mark 1:14-15] Some who lived in the first century saw the kingdom of God before they died. [Mark 9:1]

Nebuchadnezzar saw *that a stone was cut out of the mountain, without hands*, and it struck the image. **2:45,** A *mountain* represents a *kingdom*. This symbolic use of the word mountain may be found in other prophetic books of the Bible. The Lᴏʀᴅ called the kingdom of Babylon a *"destroying mountain"* in Jeremiah 51:25. Earlier, in Isaiah 2:2, the coming kingdom of God is called *"the mountain of the Lᴏʀᴅ's house."* The kingdom of God, established by Jesus Christ on the day of Pentecost, was cut out of God's eternal sovereign power. The rock was cut out without human hands. The rock is of divine origin. Jesus promised that his church (the kingdom) would be built on the rock—the truth confessed by Peter when he said to Jesus, *"You are the Christ, the Son of the living God."* [Matt. 16:16-19] Concerning this truth, Jesus said, *"flesh and blood has not revealed it unto you, but my Father which is in heaven."* The kingdom of God is built upon the rock that was cut out of God's sovereign power without human hands.

In the time of the Roman kings, God would establish a kingdom that would *"never be **destroyed**."* [2:44] Jesus promised in Matthew 16:18 that the gates of Hades will not prevail against it. Death will not overcome his church that is built upon the rock. His kingdom is eternal!

Jesus said in Mark 9:1 that the kingdom of God would *"come with power."* For forty days after his resurrection, Jesus was *"speaking of the things pertaining to the kingdom of God."* [Acts 1:3] Jesus instructed his apostles, *"You will receive power when the Holy Spirit comes on you."* [Acts 1:8, NIV] The Holy Spirit came "with power" on the day of Pentecost. [Acts 2:1-4] Thus, the kingdom of God was established on the first Pentecost after Christ's resurrection.

God had promised David that he would raise up his seed, Christ, and establish his throne forever. [2 Samuel 7:12-13] The throne of David is the throne of the LORD, according to 1 Chronicles 29:23. The power possessed by the kings of Israel was the power that God permitted them to have. [1 Samuel 12:12-15] In announcing the birth of Jesus, the angel Gabriel said to Mary, *"...the Lord God shall give unto him the throne of his father David."* [Luke 1:32] Jesus confessed that he was a king to the Roman governor Pilate and added that for this reason he was born and came into the world. [John 18:37]

Jesus was raised up from the dead to sit on the throne of David, and he is now reigning, according to Acts 2:25-36. The throne of David had been without a king for over 600 years—from the fall of Jerusalem in 586 BC to the day of Pentecost. Jesus Christ fulfills the promise made to David concerning the establishment of his throne. *"He must reign, till he has put all enemies under his feet. The last enemy that shall be destroyed is death."* [1 Cor. 15:25-26] At Christ's second coming, *"then comes the end, when he shall have delivered up the kingdom to God, even the Father; when he shall have put down all rule and all authority and power."* [1 Cor. 15:23-24]

How may we enter in the kingdom of God? Jesus said to Nicodemus, a ruler of the Jews, *"No one can enter the kingdom of God unless he is born of water and the Spirit."* [John 3:5, NIV] Jesus told Peter that he would be given *"the keys of the kingdom"* in Matthew 16:19. Peter reminded Christians that they had been *"born again . . . by the word of God that lives and abides forever."*

[1 Peter 1:23] On Pentecost, Peter was speaking the words of the Holy Spirit. [Acts 2:4] He told those who believed that Jesus is Lord and Christ to *"repent, and be baptized every one of you in the name of Jesus Christ for the remission of sins."* [Acts 2:38] The Holy Spirit works through his word to produce faith in Jesus Christ, and the new birth is completed when one is baptized— immersed in water . *"Then they that gladly received his word were baptized: and the same day there were added unto them about three thousand souls."* [Acts 2:41] This is how a person enters the kingdom of God.

The kingdom of God and the kingdom of Christ are the same. In Colossians 1:12-14, Paul gives thanks to the Father, who *"has delivered us from the power of darkness and translated us into the kingdom of his dear Son, in whom we have redemption through his blood."* The kingdom of Christ is now. If you are saved you are in it.

The kingdom of God is a spiritual kingdom. Jesus said, *"The kingdom of God does not come with your careful observation, nor will people say, 'Here it is,' or 'There it is,' because the kingdom of God is within you."* [Luke 17:20, NIV] The kingdom of God cannot be located on a map like the physical governments of this world. Jesus told Pilate, *"My kingdom is not of this world: if my kingdom were of this world, then my servants would fight, that I should not be delivered to the Jews."* Jesus came into the world to *"bear witness unto the truth."* [John 18:36, 37] Paul wrote, *"For though we live in the world, we do not wage war as the world does. The weapons we fight with are not weapons of the world. On the contrary, they have divine power to demolish strongholds. We demolish arguments and every pretension that sets itself up against the knowledge of God, and we take captive every thought to make it obedient to Christ."* [2 Cor. 10:3, 4, NIV] Jesus is not coming to set up a physical kingdom on this earth with his throne in Jerusalem. A person could say, "See, here it is!" Jesus said that the kingdom of God is not like that.

The rock that struck the statue became a huge mountain and filled the whole earth. **2:35** ^{NIV} After his resurrection, Jesus said *"that repentance and remission of sins should be preached in his name among all nations, beginning at Jerusalem."* [Luke 24:47] Repentance and remission of sins "in the name of Jesus Christ" was preached to all nations at Jerusalem on the day of Pentecost. [Acts 2:1, 5, 38] The extent of the kingdom was declared on that day when Peter said, *"For the promise is unto you, and to your children, and to all that are afar off, even as many as the Lord our God shall call."* [Acts 2:39] In giving the great commission, Jesus said, *"Go into all the world and proclaim the gospel to the whole creation. Whoever believes and is baptized will be saved."* [Mark 16:15-16, ESV]

Some promises of the Holy Spirit in the Old Testament have their fulfillment in the kingdom of God. *"Now to Abraham and his seed were the promises made. He says not. 'And to seeds,' as of many, but as of one, 'And to your seed,' which is Christ."* [Galatians 3:16] The great promise of the Bible is that all nations shall be blessed in Christ, the promised seed. [Genesis 22:18] Peter quoted this promise and said that God sent Jesus *"to bless you in turning away every one of you from your iniquities."* [Acts 3:25-26] The blessings are spiritual, not physical. A promise was made to Christ, according to Galatians 3:19. On the day of Pentecost, Jesus *"received the promise of the Holy Spirit".* [Acts 2:33] What was it? Christ received the throne of his father David and the eternal kingdom that the Holy Spirit had promised him. [Acts 2:29-35]

The great God has made known to the king what shall come to pass hereafter; and the dream is certain, and the interpretation thereof is sure. **2:45** Daniel concluded his interpretation of the dream with these words of assurance. Nebuchadnezzar's glorious kingdom would not last very long. It would fall to the Medes & Persians. This second great kingdom eventually would fall to the Greeks, and then the Romans would come to power. The purpose of the dream is to show that the eternal kingdom of God would be established in the days of the Roman Empire.

Daniel and His Companions Are Promoted
Daniel 2:46-49

Nebuchadnezzar fell on his face and said, *"Of a truth it is that your God is a God of gods, and a Lord of kings, and a revealer of secrets."* **2:46, 47** The king then promoted Daniel and gave him many great gifts. Daniel was made ruler over the whole province of Babylon and the chief administrator over all the wise men. **2:48** In response to Daniel's petition, the king also promoted Hananiah, Mishael, and Azariah, who are better known by their Babylonian names: Shadrach, Meshach, and Abed-Nego. **2:49**

Review Questions on Lesson 3

1. In Daniel 2, "God _____ Future _____."

2. Nebuchadnezzar's dream was in the _____ year of his reign.

3. How could the wise men show that they could interpret the dream? _____

4. What did the king order when his wise men failed to interpret his dream? _____

5. Who was Arioch? _____

6. After making an appointment to see the king, what did Daniel ask Hananiah, Mishael, and Azariah to do?

   _____

   _____

7. During the night the _____ was revealed.

8. In his praises of God, Daniel said, "He _____ kings and _____ kings." [2:20-21]

9. The statue in the dream had a head of _____, its chest and arms were of _____, its belly and thighs were of _____, its legs were of _____, and its feet were partly _____ and partly _____.

10. A _____ struck the statue and broke it into pieces.

11. The head of the statue represents the _____ kingdom of Nebuchadnezzar.

12. The chest and arms of silver symbolize the kingdom of the _____ & _____

13. The kingdom of _____ is the belly & thighs.

14. The kingdom of the _____ is the legs and feet.

15. What is symbolized by the feet being part of iron and part of clay? _____

16. Is the number of the statue's toes mentioned? _____

17. Daniel 2:44 predicted that in the time of the Romans, the God of heaven would set up a kingdom that would never be _____.

18. Of Jesus' kingdom "there will be no _____."

19. Jesus preached, "The time is _____and the kingdom of God is _____." [Mark 1:14-15]

20. What did some men living in the first century see before they died? [Mark 9:1] _____

21. The word *mountain* represents a _____.

22. Can the kingdom of God be located on a map? _____

23. How does a person enter the kingdom of God? [John. 3:5]
_____

Lesson 4

God Protects the Faithful from Fire
Daniel 3

Nebuchadnezzar the king made an image of gold, whose height was sixty cubits and the breadth thereof was six cubits; he set it up in the plain of Dura in the province of Babylon. **3:1** A cubit of 18 inches would make the statue 90 feet tall and 9 feet wide. Liberal scholars criticize this description saying that such a tall yet narrow image would be ugly due to its disproportionate dimensions. However, it is most likely that the image was on a base or pedestal like our Statue of Liberty. The plain of Dura was near the city of Babylon, but the exact location is uncertain. Southeast of Babylon in the vicinity of the mounds of *Duair*, the pedestal of a huge statue has been found.[25] The statue may have been of Nebuchadnezzar himself. He was the golden head of the great statue in the dream that Daniel interpreted. [2:38] As we shall see later in this story, Nebuchadnezzar thought he was greater than any god. [3:15]

The king sent to gather together the princes, the governors (and the various other government officials) *to the dedication of the image.* **3:2** Since nothing is said about Daniel, we assume that he was not there for the dedication. Shadrach, Meshach, and Abed-Nego had been appointed administrators in the government [2:49], and they were present. Daniel was in charge of the wise men. [2:48] He was an academic official. [4:9] What an impressive sight! The enormous statue of dazzling gold! The great assembly of government officials!

---

[25] F. N. Peloubet, *Peloubet's Bible Dictionary*, "Dura", p. 155

Then the herald cried out: *"To you it is commanded ... that at what time you hear the sound of the cornet, flute, harp, sackbut, psaltery, dulcimer, and all kinds of music, you fall down and worship the golden image that Nebuchadnezzar the king has set up. And who so falls not down and worships shall the same hour be cast into the midst of a burning fiery furnace."* 3:4-6 While the music was playing, everyone was bowing down and worshiping the image — except Daniel's three friends.

Certain Chaldeans came before the king and accused Shadrach, Meshach, and Abed-Nego for not serving his gods or worshiping his golden image. **3:8-12** Earlier, these young men had not defiled themselves with the king's food. Now, they refused to defile themselves with the king's religion. There will always be those who will accuse the righteous because of their envy and jealousy.

Nebuchadnezzar was in a furious rage when he learned that the three young men refused to worship his image, and he commanded that they be brought in to appear before him. **3:13** This was a **double test** for them. First, they knew the king had the power and the disposition to kill them. [2:5, 12] On the other hand, Nebuchadnezzar had treated them kindly and had promoted them in his government. Jim McGuiggan observes, "It's often harder to oppose one who has been kind to you than one who's terribly angry with you."

The king had been impressed by these young men. [1:19-20] He did not want to kill them, so he controlled his anger and gave them another chance to worship his image. He was saying in effect, "Please, just do it, and all will be well with you." **3:14-15**

Think how they could have rationalized their situation and yielded to the temptation. Everyone is doing it; I don't want to be different. I am just a youth; God will overlook a youthful indiscretion. We are only three; what can three do? If we don't worship the image, we will be killed; but if we do, we can live and be useful to God for many years. Besides, we know the image is nothing, and true worship takes place in the heart, so we can just go through the motions of bowing to the image with our fingers crossed. The question facing them (and us) is—Shall we live by our faith or shall we lie to ourselves and make excuses.

Then the king challenged the foundation of their faith, saying, *"Who is that God that shall deliver you out of my hands?"* **3:15** He sounded like Pharaoh of Egypt, who said, "Who is the LORD, that I should obey his voice?" [Exodus 5:2] He reminds us of Sennacherib king of Assyria, who said to Hezekiah king of Judah, "Let not your God in whom you trust deceive you...Have the gods of the nations delivered them which my fathers have destroyed?" [2 Kings 19:10, 12] These kings are like "the beast" of Revelation 13:1-6, who "opened his mouth in blasphemy against God."

Shadrach, Meshach, and Abed-Nego did not hesitate to answer the king. They boldly declared, *"Our God whom we serve is able to deliver us from the burning fiery furnace, and he will deliver us out of your hand, O King."* **3:17** God would deliver them either physically from the blazing furnace or spiritually. Even in death,

God would give them the victory! *"If God be for us, who can be against us?"* [Romans 8:31, 36-39]

The young men added, ***"But if not, be it known unto you, O King, that we will not serve your gods, nor worship the golden image which you have set up."*** **3:18** No more courageous words of faith were ever spoken. Their words were plainly stated. No one could misunderstand them. We should not be ashamed of our faith. Others should know where we stand.

Shadrach, Meshach, and Abed-Nego had the spiritual strength to face the favors and the threats of a powerful and cruel king because they had faith in the living God of heaven. They believed the words of Habakkuk 2:20, *"The LORD is in his holy temple: let all the earth keep silence before him."* They knew the Most High is the one who rules the kingdom of men. They did not fear those who kill the body but cannot kill the soul. Rather, they feared him which is able to destroy both soul and body in hell. [Matthew 10:28] They were bowing before a greater King on a greater throne. We need this kind of faith in the time of temptation, and we need to remember that God protects the faithful from fire. He can protect us from the everlasting fire of hell. [Matthew 25:41]

Nebuchadnezzar had been controlling his temper, but he lost all restraint, and he let go of his wrath. His facial expression changed; he became furious. How dare they talk to the king of Babylon in this way! He ordered that the heat of the furnace be increased seven times. **3:19** Then he commanded the most mighty men in his army to bind these three young men and cast them into the furnace. **3:20**

But the fire was so hot that it killed the strong soldiers as they threw Shadrach, Meshach, and Abed-Nego into the furnace. **3:22** There was no question about the heat and the reality of the flames.

Then Nebuchadnezzar stood up and asked his officials, *"Weren't there three men that we tied up and threw into the fire? Look! I see four men walking around in the fire, unbound and unharmed, and the fourth looks like a son of the gods."* **3:24-25** ᴺᴵⱽ The fury of the king had been changed into amazement. He turned from his arrogant blasphemy to humble praise for the God of heaven.

As Nebuchadnezzar approached the furnace he called out, *"Shadrach, Meshach, and Abed-Nego, servants of the Most High God, come out! Come here!"* **3:26** ᴺᴵⱽ When they came out, everyone saw that these young men had not been harmed by the fire. The hair on their heads had not been singed; their clothing had not been scorched, and there was no burnt smell on them. [3:27] Nebuchadnezzar then praised the true God of heaven, *"who has sent his angel, and delivered his servants that trusted in him, and have changed the king's word, and yielded their bodies, that they might not serve nor worship any god except their own God."* [3:28] Others take notice when we live by our faith.

Nebuchadnezzar was so impressed by the power of God that he proclaimed, *"Therefore I make a decree that every people, nation, and language, which speak anything amiss against the God of Shadrach, Meshach and Abed-Nego shall be cut in pieces and their houses shall be made a dunghill, because there is no other god that can deliver after this sort."* **3:29** He sounds like a Mafia boss expressing religious convictions. This proud and violent man was learning more about the true God in heaven.

The earth was beginning to be filled with the knowledge of the glory of the LORD, just as God had promised in Habakkuk 2:14. If these young men had not lived by their faith, the king would not have made this decree. Faith changes things!

Then the king promoted Shadrach, Meshach, and Abed-Nego in the province of Babylon. **3:30** But from this story, they seemed to be more interested in God's approval. We are exhorted in 2 Timothy 2:15, *"Be diligent to present yourself approved to God."* NKJV

Jesus promises, *"He that overcomes shall not be hurt by the second death"* which is *"the lake of fire".* [Revelation 2:11, Revelation 20:14]

Indeed, God does protect the faithful from fire.

Review Questions on Lesson 4

1. "God _____ the Faithful from _____."

2. Nebuchadnezzar made a statue of _____ that was _____ feet high and _____ feet wide and set it up in the plain of _____. [3:1]

3. When they heard the sound of all kinds of musical instruments, what was everyone to do? [3:5]

   _____

   _____

4. Who would be thrown into a fiery, blazing furnace?

   _____

5. What three persons were accused of not worshiping?

   _____

6. Earlier, these three had not been defiled with the king's _____, and now they refused to be defiled with the king's _____ [cf. Daniel 1:11-16]

7. What was the king's immediate response?

   _____

8. Why did the king want to give them a second chance?

   _____

9. What was the "double test" for them?
   (1) _____
   (2) _____

10. Shall we live by our _____ or shall we _____ to ourselves and make excuses?

11. What question did the king ask that challenged the faith of these young men and showed his arrogance? [3:15]

    _____

    _____

12. They replied, "Our God whom we serve is _____
    _____."

13. They stated, "We will not serve _____ _____,
    nor _____ the golden image which you
    have set up."

14. What then did the king command? _____
    _____
    _____

15. What happened to the strong soldiers that carried out
    the king's command? _____

16. What did the king see when he looked into the furnace?
    _____
    _____

17. The king called Shadrach, Meshach, and Abed-Nego
    "Servants of the _____ _____ God".

18. The king made a decree stating that "no other god can
    _____ in this way."

19. What did the king do to Shadrach, Meshach, and Abed-
    Nego? _____

20. Jesus promises that the one who overcomes shall not be
    hurt by the second death, which is the lake of _____.

Lesson 5

God Humbles a Proud King
Daniel 4

Nebuchadnezzar the king, unto all people, nations, and languages that dwell in all the earth: Peace be multiplied unto you. **4:1** This chapter was written by Nebuchadnezzar in his own language. From Daniel 2:4 through 7:28, the book is in Aramaic, the language of the Chaldeans. Daniel had been taught this language. [1:4]

The king begins with praise for the Most High God. *How great are his signs! And how mighty are his wonders! His kingdom is an everlasting kingdom, and his dominion is from generation to generation.* **4:2-3**

I Nebuchadnezzar was at rest in mine house and flourishing in my palace. **4:4** He did not fear any enemy, for the walls of the city of Babylon were over 300 feet high and over 80 feet wide.[26] The king's palace was protected by several walls that ranged from 20 to 50 feet in thickness. But the God of heaven could get to Nebuchadnezzar through a dream that made this proud king tremble with fear. **4:5**

The king commanded that all his wise men be brought before him, but they could not interpret his dream. **4:6-7** After the others had failed, Daniel at last came before Nebuchadnezzar, and the king told him his dream. **4:8-18**

Nebuchadnezzar saw *a tree in the midst of the earth, and the height thereof was great. The tree grew and became strong.* **4:10, 11** Its height reached to the sky,

---

[26] *International Standard Bible Encyclopaedia*

and it could be seen to the ends of the earth. Its leaves were beautiful, and it was loaded with fruit. The tree provided food and shelter for all. Then a holy one from heaven called with a loud voice: ***"Hew down the tree . . . Nevertheless, leave the stump*** *of his roots in the earth, even with a band of iron and brass . . . and let it be wet with the dew of heaven, and let **his** portion be with the beasts in the grass of the earth."* The tree is a person; notice the pronouns **his** and **him.** *"Let **his** heart be changed from man's, and let a beast's heart be given* **him,** *and let seven times pass over* **him** *. . .* ***to the intent that the living may know that the Most High rules in the kingdom of men, and gives it to whomsoever he will, and sets up over it the basest of men."*** 4:14-17 God can rule through anyone to accomplish his purpose. (We should not be too stirred up over politics.)

Daniel hesitated to tell the king the meaning of his dream because its message was one the king would not welcome. The king assured Daniel that he was willing to hear the interpretation regardless of how unpleasant it might be. Daniel prepared the king for the worst by saying, ***"My lord,*** (may) ***the dream be to them that hate you, and the interpretation to your enemies."*** 4:19 But such was not the case.

"It is you, O King, that have grown and become strong: for your greatness is grown, and reaches unto heaven, and your dominion to the end of the earth." 4:22

But the king would be driven away from people and live with the animals of the field and eat grass with the cattle. The command to leave ***the stump*** of the tree meant that his kingdom would be restored to him when he acknowledged that the Most High rules in the kingdom of men. **4:24-26** God has the power to preserve the kingdom of Babylon even while its king is insane and living with the animals. This is symbolized by the iron and bronze guard around the stump.

Daniel concluded, *"Wherefore, O king, let my counsel be acceptable unto you, and break off your sins by righteousness, and your iniquities by showing mercy to the poor, if it may be a lengthening of your tranquility."* **4:27** Over two hundred years earlier, God had spared the city of Nineveh when its king and people repented. However, Nebuchadnezzar did not accept Daniel's advice at this time.

The dream was fulfilled twelve months later. The king probably had forgotten the warnings of the dream. Because God does not punish immediately, we also may forget his warnings in the Bible. *"The Lord is not slack concerning his promise, as some men count slackness; but is longsuffering to us, not willing that any should perish, but that all should come to repentance."* [2 Peter 3:9] As Nebuchadnezzar was walking on the roof of his palace in Babylon, he said, *"Is not this great Babylon that I have built for the house of the kingdom by the might of my power, and for the honor of my majesty?"* **4:29-30** Nebuchadnezzar's Hanging Gardens were one of the seven wonders of the ancient world, according to the Greeks.

Before the king had finished his last word, a voice from heaven began speaking. *"O king Nebuchadnezzar, to you it is spoken: The kingdom is departed from you.*

And they shall drive you from men, and your dwelling shall be with the beasts of the field." **4:31-32** There is a mental disorder in which a person thinks and acts like an animal; it is a form of insanity. *"Pride goes before destruction, and a haughty spirit before a fall."* [Proverbs 16:18]

The heavenly messenger informed Nebuchadnezzar, *"seven times shall pass over you until you know that the Most High rules in the kingdom of men."* **4:32** Some think the seven times are seven years. Others think the seven times are seven seasons of only summer and winter, which would be three-and-a-half years. Still others say that the seven times is symbolic of whatever time is needed for him to acknowledge that the Most High is the supreme ruler of the earth. In one of his inscriptions Nebuchadnezzar wrote: "For four years the residence of my kingdom did not delight my heart." [27] He was more interested in eating grass with the cattle.

God's judgments come quickly and unexpectedly. The prophecy concerning Nebuchadnezzar was fulfilled within an hour. *And he was driven from men, and did eat grass as oxen, and his body was wet with the dew of heaven, till his hairs were grown like eagle's feathers, and his nails like birds' claws.* **4:33**

The king tells of his humbling experience. *"And at the end of the days, I, Nebuchadnezzar, lifted up my eyes unto heaven, and my understanding returned to me; and I blessed the Most High and I praised and honored him that lives forever, whose dominion is an*

---

[27] Henry H. Halley, *Bible Handbook*, Daniel, p. 30

everlasting dominion, and his kingdom is from generation to generation. And all the inhabitants of the earth are reputed as nothing, and he does according to his will in the army of heaven and among the inhabitants of the earth; and none can stay his hand, or say unto him, 'What are you doing?'" 4:34-35

After God restored to him his sanity and the kingdom, Nebuchadnezzar praised the King of heaven, whose works are truth and whose ways are justice. The knowledge of the glory of the LORD was spread over the entire world. This once proud king closes his letter to all the inhabitants of the earth with this humble acknowledgement: *"And those that walk in pride he is able to abase."* 4:37

Review Questions on Lesson 5

1. Daniel 4, "God _____ a _____ King."

2. Who wrote Daniel 4? _____

3. What is the significance of Daniel 4 being written in the Aramaic language? _____
_____

4. The king had a dream that made him _____.

5. What did the king see in his dream? _____

6. What command was given? [v. 14] _____

7. How do we know the dream is about a person? _____
_____

8. The heart (or mind) of the person represented by the tree would be changed into that of _____.

9. What was the purpose of the dream? [4:17] _____
_____
_____

10. Who was able to interpret the dream? _____

11. The great tree represented _____.

12. What would happen to the king? _____
_____

13. What is the meaning of "leave the stump"? _____
_____

14. What was Daniel's advice to Nebuchadnezzar? _____
_____

15. Did the king accept his advice? _____

16. The dream was fulfilled twelve _____ later.

17. Why does God delay his punishment of sin? [2 Pet. 3:9]
_____

18. Nebuchadnezzar's _____ _____
was one of "The Seven Wonders of the Ancient
World".

19. What had the king just said when the voice from heaven
told him that his kingdom had departed from him?
_____
_____
_____

20. What are three explanations for the "seven times"?
(1) _____
(2) _____
(3) _____

21. Nebuchadnezzar's _____ returned
to him at the end of the time. [4:34]

22. What did the king do? [4:34] _____
_____

23. What also was restored to him? _____

24. He praised the God of heaven, saying, "And those who
walk in pride he is able to _____."

NOTES

Lesson 6

God Judges the Kingdom of Babylon
Daniel 5

Daniel is now over 80 years old, and Belshazzar is king. The year is 539 BC.

Belshazzar was unknown in the Babylonian records until 1853. Nabonidus (Nab-o-<u>ne</u>-dus) was known as the last king of Babylon. "But in 1853 an inscription was found in a cornerstone of a temple built by Nabonidus...which read, 'Belshazzar, my firstborn, my favorite son.'" [28] Another discovery is reported by Edward J. Young in the following: "It is stated on one text ... that Nabonidus entrusted the kingship to his son Belshazzar, and that he himself established his dwelling in Tema (in Arabia). Furthermore, Belshazzar is spoken of in such a way as to show that he did exercise regal functions ... Oaths are taken in the name of both men. Thus we read, 'The decrees of Nabonidus king of Babylon and Belshazzar, the son of the king.' Belshazzar grants leases, issues commands, performs an administrative act concerning the temple at Erech, possesses subordinate officials which are equal to those of the king ... In addition, it must be remembered that the Aramaic word translated 'king' need not have the connotation of absolute monarch." [29] The fact that Belshazzar was a co-regent with his father is established by Belshazzar's offer to make someone "the **third** highest ruler in the kingdom." [Daniel 5:7, 16, 29]

---

[28] Henry H. Halley, *Bible Handbook*, Daniel 5
[29] Edward J. Young, *An Introduction to the Old Testament*, p. 388

Belshazzar the king made a feast to a thousand of his lords and drank wine. **5:1** King Belshazzar hosted a great banquet for a thousand of his nobles, and they were drinking wine together. The army of the Medes & Persians was camped outside the city. But the Babylonians felt secure behind their strong, high walls. They had plenty of food and provisions. Water was provided by the Euphrates River that ran under the city walls and up to it. The river flowed through the middle of the city with protective walls on both sides. With arrogant confidence, the king was having a drunken party in honor of his gods. [5:4]

Belshazzar, while he tasted the wine, commanded to bring the golden and silver vessels which his father Nebuchadnezzar had taken out of the temple which was in Jerusalem; that the king, and his princes, his wives, and his concubines might drink. **5:2** "Apparently Belshazzar was lineally related to Nebuchadnezzar because his mother, Nitrocris, seems to have been Nebuchadnezzar's daughter." [30] Nebuchadnezzar is called "his father" although he was his grandfather. "Father" is used to mean ancestor. In the same way, David is called the father of Jesus in Matthew 1:1 and Luke 1:32. The king and his nobles with his wives and concubines drank wine from the holy vessels and praised their gods. **5:3, 4**

In the same hour came forth fingers of a man's hand, and wrote ... upon the plaster of the wall of the king's palace. **5:5** The king's face became pale with fright. He was so troubled in his mind that he began to tremble, and his knees knocked together. **5:6**

---

[30] *The New Unger's Bible Dictionary,* "Belshazzar"

Belshazzar called for his wise men to be brought in. He said, *"Whosoever shall read this writing and show me the interpretation thereof shall be clothed with scarlet, and have a chain of gold about his neck, and shall be the third ruler in the kingdom."* **5:7** But none of them could do it. So the king became more frightened and terrified. **5:8, 9**

Then the queen entered the banquet hall and told the king about Daniel. **5:10-12** Since Belshazzar's wives were already at the banquet [5:3], "the queen" must be the wife of Nabonidus and the mother of Belshazzar. She knew Daniel when he interpreted the dreams of her father, Nebuchadnezzar. So Daniel was brought before the king. **5:13-16**

Daniel was not interested in the king's rewards, but he wanted the king to know God's message for him. **5:17** He began by reviewing the history of the kingdom of Babylon. *"The most high God gave Nebuchadnezzar your father a kingdom and majesty and glory and honor ... But when his heart was lifted up, and his mind hardened in pride, he was deposed from his kingly throne, and they took his glory from him."* **5:18, 20** This is a reference to the events in Daniel 4. *"And you his son, O Belshazzar, have not humbled your heart, though you knew all this."* **5:22** Belshazzar knew how the God of heaven had humbled his grandfather and had proved to him that the Most High rules in the kingdom of men. Instead of honoring the true God, Belshazzar profaned his holy vessels. Are we living our lives according to the knowledge that we have of God?

Daniel then revealed God's accusation against the king: *"You have exalted yourself against the Lord of heaven."* **5:23** ^{NASB} Belshazzar profaned the holy vessels from the temple of God by misusing them. If we misuse our bodies or profane the Lord's church, we are doing the same thing, because we are the holy temple of God today. [1 Cor. 6:19, 20] Daniel concluded the accusation with these words: *"But you did not honor the God who holds in his hand your life and all your ways."* **5:23** ^{NIV}

This is the interpretation of the handwriting on the wall:
MENE means *numbered.*
"God has **numbered** your kingdom and finished it."
TEKEL means *weighed.*
"You are **weighed** in the balances, and are found wanting."
PERES means *divided.*
"Your kingdom is **divided** and given to the Medes and Persians."
5:25-28

The word on the wall was UPHARSIN, the plural form of the word PERES. The Babylonian kingdom would be smashed into bits, many pieces, and not simply divided.

For his interpreting of the handwriting on the wall, *they clothed Daniel with scarlet, and put a chain of gold about his neck, and made a proclamation concerning him, that he should be the third ruler in the kingdom.* **5:29** But what good is it to be third ruler of a kingdom that would not see another day? *In that night was Belshazzar the king of the Chaldeans slain.* **5:30**

These events had been predicted at least 150 years earlier by the prophet Isaiah.

The thirteenth chapter of Isaiah is about the fall of Babylon. *"The day of the* LORD *is at hand; it shall come as a destruction from the Almighty . . . Behold, I will stir up the Medes against them . . . And Babylon . . . shall never be inhabited . . . But wild beasts of the desert shall lie there."* [Isaiah 13:6, 17, 19, 20, 21] Homer Hailey explains the destruction of the city. "One might infer from this that the destruction would be immediate, but this is not the case. Delitzch says that Cyrus left the city still standing with its double ring of walls. 'Darius Hystaspis, who had to conquer Babylon a second time in 518 BC, had the walls entirely destroyed. . . . Having been conquered by Seleucus Nicator (312), it declined. ... At the time of Strabo (born 60 BC), Babylon was a perfect desert.' . . . So although not immediately, the prophecy was totally fulfilled."[31] Don Shackelford observes, "It is interesting that the site of Babylon has never again been inhabited since its destruction. Today, its only occupants are desert creatures, owls, ostriches, shaggy goats, hyenas, and jackals!" [32]

Belshazzar's banquet and drinking party on that fateful night is described in Isaiah 21. God gives the command, *"Go up, O Elam: besiege, O Media."* [v. 2] "Elam was a province of Persia. The name Persia was not in use until the captivity. It is a mark of authenticity that the name is not found before Daniel and Ezekiel." [33]

---

[31] Homer Hailey, *A Commentary on Isaiah*, p. 135
[32] Don Shackelford, *Truth for Today Commentary, Isaiah*, p. 177
[33] *Jamieson, Fausset, and Brown Commentary*, Isaiah 21:2

Cyrus, the founder of the Persian Empire, was from eastern Elam with Susa as its capital.[34] Isaiah 21:2 is predicting that the Persians and the Medes would go up against Babylon and besiege the city. The Lord would bring to an end all of the suffering she had caused his people. This is essentially the same message as the handwriting on the wall in Daniel 5. Isaiah can feel the pain and terror of Belshazzar as he learned of his doom. *"I am staggered by what I hear; I am bewildered by what I see. My heart falters, fear makes me tremble; the twilight I longed for has become a horror to me."* [Isaiah 21:3-4, NIV] According to Albert Barnes, "There can be no doubt that the prophet here refers to the night of revelry and riot in which Babylon was taken." [35] That evening is summed up in verse five: *"Prepare the table* (the banquet), *watch in the watchtower* (the enemy is outside the gates), *eat, drink:* (and after the Lord's handwriting, the order is given) *arise you princes, and anoint the shield* (for battle)." Then the watchman cried out: *"Babylon is fallen, is fallen."* [Isaiah 21:9)]

How Babylon fell is predicted in Isaiah 44. *"I am the Lord that says to the deep, 'Be dry, and I will dry up your rivers:' that says of Cyrus, 'He is my shepherd and shall perform all my pleasure.'"* [verses 24, 27, 28] Barnes tells us, "Cyrus took Babylon by diverting the waters of the river Euphrates, and thus leaving the bed of the river dry, so that he could march his army under the walls of the city." [36]

---

[34] *Nelson's Illustrated Bible Dictionary*, Elam
[35] Albert Barnes, *Barnes' Notes*, Isaiah 21
[36] Albert Barnes, *Barnes' Notes*, Isaiah 44

And Darius the Mede received the kingdom, being about sixty-two years old. **5:31** ^{NKJV} Daniel said that Darius *"was made king over the realm of the Chaldeans."* [9:1]

Who was Darius the Mede? He is unknown in secular history like Belshazzar, who was unknown for over 2300 years. Just because historians don't know about him, does not mean that he did not exist. Perhaps his name also will be found in some future archeological discovery. We must keep in mind that the Bible is an inspired history book, and its trustworthiness has been proven again and again. Even the Greek historians, Herodotus (484-424 BC) and Xenophon (434-355 BC) do not agree about how Cyrus came to power. Bradford Welles gives these words of caution concerning Herodotus: "He even included many stories which he did not believe, because they made his account more interesting." [37]   Xenophon served as a soldier under Cyrus II and had firsthand knowledge of Persian history. He tells us that the king of the Medes at the time of the fall of Babylon was Cyaxares II.

Darius the Mede may have been known by another name, just like Esther's king Ahasuerus was also known as Xerxes by world historians. Several attempts have been made to identify Darius the Mede with someone who was living at the time of the fall of Babylon. Cyaxares II seems to be the most likely one. He was a brother of Cyrus' mother, thus making him Cyrus' uncle.

[37] *The World Book Encyclopedia*, Vol. 9, p. 199, 1974 edition

Cyrus became king of a Persian tribe in 559 BC. About five years later he was king over all of Persia.[38] While his uncle Cyaxares II was reigning over Media, Cyrus served as the general of the united army of the Medes & Persians in defeating the Lydian king Croesus in 546 BC. Cyrus' army conquered Babylon in 539 BC. Cyrus entered the city of Babylon on October 29 and proclaimed peace. As governor of Babylon, Gobryas had installed sub-governors before he died on November 6, just a few days later. [39] Xenophon provides the following information: "After the conquest of Babylon, the army regarded Cyrus as king. But he went however to Media, to present himself before Cyaxares. He brought presents to him, and showed him that there was a house and palace ready for him in Babylon, where he might reside. Cyaxares gave him his daughter to wife, and along with her, as a dowry, the whole of Media, for he had no son." This is how Cyrus became king over Media as well as Persia.

Darius the Mede could well be Cyaxares, because he was sixty-two years old, old enough to be Cyrus' uncle. Cyrus needed someone to replace Gobryas, who had been governor of Babylon. Darius the Mede was chosen as king of Babylon, not governor, for he had been the king of Media.

"Cyrus was the supreme king and conqueror, and Darius made subordinate king under him. It is probable that this Darius was representative of the deposed Median line of supreme kings...and that Cyrus deemed it politic to give him a share of royal power, in order to

---

[38] Edward McNall Burns, *Western Civilizations*, p. 65,
[39] *Nabonidus Chronicle*, Year 17, translations by A. Leo Oppenheim

consolidate by union the two dynasties and conciliate the Medes. Darius reigned as viceroy at Babylon from 538 to 536 B.C., when Cyrus assumed the throne there himself; from whence Ezra [Ezra 1:1] regards the year of Cyrus' beginning to reign at Babylon as the first year of his reign over the whole empire, though he was king of Persia 20 years before." [40]

Keil & Delitzsch agree with Xenophon's account and show that it agrees with the Scriptures. "The supposition that Darius reigned for two years over Babylon is correct." [41]

The exile was to last seventy years, according to Jeremiah 29:10. In the first year of Cyrus, he made a decree that fulfilled this prophecy of Jeremiah, according to Ezra 1:1. In 606 BC, the first captives were taken to Babylon, and Babylon fell to the Medes & Persians in 539 BC, only sixty-seven or sixty-eight years later. Cyrus did not free the Jews immediately after he conquered Babylon, because the seventy years were not completed. Daniel wrote chapter nine "in the first year of Darius", and the Jews were still in captivity. [9:1] Daniel wrote chapter ten "in the third year of Cyrus." [10:1] "Daniel prospered in the reign of Darius and in the reign of Cyrus," according to Daniel 6:28. Those are two separate reigns. In 536 BC, Cyrus began to reign at Babylon and made his decree for the Jews to return to Jerusalem after seventy years of captivity. Trust the Bible's account of history.

---

[40] *Fausset's Bible Dictionary*, "Cyrus", Biblesoft
[41] *Keil & Delitzsch Commentary on the Old Testament*, Daniel 6:1-8

Review Questions on Lesson 6

1. Daniel 5, "God _____ the Kingdom of Babylon."

2. Until 1853, Nabonidus was known as the last king of Babylon, and _____ was unknown.

3. One text states that Nabonidus entrusted the kingship to his son _____ while he was in Arabia.

4. The year was _____ BC and Daniel was over _____ years old.

5. King Belshazzar gave a _____ for his nobles and drank _____ and praised his _____ .

6. Where was the army of the Medes and Persians?

   _____

   _____

7. What made the king feel secure?_____

   _____

   _____

   _____

8. When Nebuchadnezzar is called Belshazzar's father, the word "father" means _____ .

9. How did the king misuse the vessels from God's temple in Jerusalem?_____

   _____

10. Where were Belshazzar's wives at this time? [5:2-3]

   _____

11. What appeared on the wall of the banquet hall? [5:5]

   _____

12. What was promised to the one who could interpret the writing?_____
_____

13. Who told the king about Daniel? _____
_____

14. After telling how God had humbled Nebuchadnezzar, Daniel said, "But you his son, Belshazzar, have not _____ your heart, although you _____ all this." [5:22]

15. "But you did not _____ the God who holds in his hand your _____ and all your _____." [5:23, NIV]

16. MENE means _____.
    TEKEL means _____.
    PERES means _____.

17. "God has _____ your kingdom and finished it. You have been _____ in the balances and found wanting. Your kingdom has been _____ and given to the Medes and Persians."

18. That very night Belshazzar was _____. [5:30]

19. Who took over the kingdom? _____

20. Who had predicted these events over 150 years earlier?
_____

NOTES

Lesson 7

God Delivers Daniel from the Lions
Daniel 6

The kingdom of the Medes & Persians had two kings. [8:20] Cyrus the king of Persia was the military genius who planned the attack on Babylon and continued his conquests after defeating the Chaldeans. Eventually the kingdom of the Medes & Persians was about three times the size of Nebuchadnezzar's kingdom. At the age of 62, Darius the Mede began ruling in the city of Babylon over what had been the Chaldean kingdom. [5:31, 9:1] He appointed Daniel to be one of the three chief officials,[42] to whom 120 satraps were accountable. **6:1, 2**

Because of his excellent spirit and exceptional qualities, Daniel stood out from among the others. When King Darius started making plans to set Daniel over the whole realm, the other chief officials and satraps became envious of him. They could not find any corruption or negligence in his work. But they did notice that Daniel was devoted to his God. Therefore, they persuaded Darius to issue a decree that anyone who prayed to any god except the king during the next thirty days would be thrown into a den of lions. **6:3-9**

Although Daniel knew about the king's decree, he went home and prayed as he had done since coming to Babylon as a teenager — three times a day on his knees, looking toward Jerusalem. **6:10** God had promised to hear the prayers of his people even in a foreign land when they prayed toward the city of Jerusalem. [1 Kings 8:48]

---

[42] The Hebrew word for Daniel's office is "chief or overseer" according to *Brown-Driver-Brigg's Hebrew Lexicon*.

Daniel knew that the laws of men cannot change the law of God, and he chose *"to obey God rather than men."* [Acts 5:29] Daniel was not making a "show" of prayer. Praying regularly in his home had been his practice long before the king made his decree. Jesus warns us about praying to be seen by men in Matthew 6:5-6.

Daniel's enemies found him praying and giving thanks to God. They reported Daniel's actions to the king and reminded him of his decree. **6:11-13** ***Then the king ... was sore displeased with himself, and set his heart on Daniel to deliver him.*** **6:14** But he could not, because the law of the Medes and Persians was that no decree could be changed. **6:15** King Darius was humbled; his pride had caused him to do something he regretted. Sometimes a wrong decision cannot be undone. Because the decree was unchangeable, the king had to give the order for Daniel to be thrown into the den of lions. **6:16**

The king showed his faith in the true God by saying, ***"Your God whom you serve continually, he will deliver you."*** **6:16** No doubt Daniel had told Darius about God, and how he had revealed his power to Nebuchadnezzar and to Belshazzar. The predictions Daniel made on the night when Babylon fell to the Medes and Persians may explain why Daniel was given such a high position in the new government.

A stone was placed on the mouth of the den of lions, and the king sealed it with his own signet. **6:17** This was done to prevent any attempt of rescue. We know that Daniel spent the night with the lions. A seal is a symbol of the authority behind it, such as the seal of the United States or a state seal on a birth certificate. If anyone moved the stone, he would have to answer to the king. A crime scene is "sealed off" to keep unauthorized people out.

Although the king returned to his palace, he could not eat or sleep that night. **6:18**

As it began to dawn in the morning, he got up and hurried to the den of lions. He was eager to know if Daniel had survived the night. He called out, *"Daniel, servant of the living God, is your God, whom you serve continually, able to deliver you from the lions?"* **6:20** He showed his respect for God by acknowledging him as "the living God."

Daniel answered, *"My God has sent his angel and has shut the lions' mouths, that they have not hurt me."* **6:22** Angels are called "ministering spirits" in Hebrews 1:14. In Hebrews 11:32-33 we read of *"the prophets: who through faith subdued kingdoms, wrought righteousness, obtained promises, stopped the mouths of lions."* This story is confirmed by the New Testament.

Darius was exceedingly glad that Daniel was alive, and he commanded that he be removed from the lions' den. Daniel had not been injured in any way. *So Daniel was taken up out of the den, and no manner of hurt was found upon him, because he believed in his God."* **6:23** Again we are reminded that the just shall live by faith. [Habakkuk 2:4]

Then the king commanded that the enemies of Daniel be thrown into the den of lions. Jesus taught, *"For with*

what judgment you judge, you shall be judged."
[Matthew 7:2] The lions overpowered these wicked men
before they reached the floor of the den. **6:24** This
proves that these were ferocious lions.

The king then praised God with a decree that he sent
to all the peoples and nations of the earth. **6:25-27** The
earth was filled with the knowledge of the glory of God.

And Daniel did well in the reign of Darius the Mede
and during the reign of Cyrus the Persian. **6:28** After
years of conquests, Cyrus became king over the entire
Persian Empire in 536 BC. This fulfilled the prophecy
of Daniel 8:3, 20.

Introduction to Daniel 7 – 12

The prophecies of Daniel are in chapters seven
through twelve. The four major visions are as follows:

> The Four Beasts, Chapter 7
> The Ram and the Goat, Chapter 8
> The Seventy Weeks, Chapter 9
> The Latter Days of the Jews, Chapters 10-12

These prophecies were revealed during the time covered
in the first six chapters. In chapter seven, Daniel relates
a dream he had during the first year of Belshazzar's
reign. [7:1] In chapter eight, the vision of "The Ram
and the Goat" was during Belshazzar's third year as
king. [8:1] Daniel saw the vision of "The Seventy
Weeks" during the first year of Darius king of the
Medes. [9:1, 24] A vision was revealed to Daniel about
"The Latter Days of the Jews" in the third year of Cyrus
king of Persia. [10:1, 14]

Prophetic scriptures are highly figurative. They do not have to be interpreted literally to be true. A **symbol** is a representation which stands for something else. The symbol of the *"wind"* in Daniel 7:2 refers to God's action. When the Lord established the kingdom of God on the day of Pentecost there was *"a sound from heaven as of a rushing mighty wind."* [Acts 2:1-2] The *sea* in Daniel 7:2 is a symbol of the ungodly nations in a restless condition. *"Woe to the multitude of many people, which make a noise like the noise of the seas; and to the rushing of nations, that make a rushing like the rushing of mighty waters! The nations shall rush like the rushing of many waters: but God shall rebuke them."* [Isaiah 17:12, 13]

Three Rules for Interpreting Symbols

(1) **If the writer interprets the symbol, accept it.** This rule was used to interpret "the head of gold" in Daniel 2:38.

(2) **See how other writers use and interpret the symbol.** This rule was used to explain the symbols in Daniel 7:2.

(3) **A symbol may be used in different ways to represent different things.** "Leaven" (yeast) is used to show the positive influence of the kingdom of heaven in Matthew 13:33, but it also may represent a bad influence as in 1 Cor. 5:6-8. Leaven represents influence, good or bad.

Two Major Interpretations of Prophecy

The premillennial interpretation states that Christ will return to earth **before** the thousand years mentioned in Revelation 20. The name comes from the prefix *pre* meaning "before" and *millennial* referring to a "thousand years." According to this view, Jesus will establish his kingdom at his second coming and reign on earth in the city of Jerusalem for a literal thousand years.

The symbolic millennial interpretation says that the thousand years of Revelation 20 are **symbolic** and that Christ will return **after** their fulfillment. Premillennialists incorrectly refer to this view as *amillennialism*. An atheist is a person who denies the existence of God. Thus, an *amillennialist* would be one who denies the thousand years of Revelation 20. Those who do not agree with a literal interpretation are not denying the truth of Revelation 20 when they interpret the thousand years as being symbolic. This view teaches that Christ established his spiritual kingdom, the church, on the day of Pentecost following his death, burial, and resurrection. He is now reigning on God's throne in heaven. [See Daniel 7:13-14 and Acts 2:29-36.]

Review Questions on Lesson 7

1. Daniel 6, "God _____ Daniel from the Lions."

2. Darius the _____ began ruling over what had been the Chaldean kingdom in Babylon.

3. Cyrus the _____ was the military genius who continued his conquests for the next two or three years.

4. Darius made Daniel one of _____ chief officials to whom _____ satraps were accountable.

5. The other chief officials and satraps became _____ of Daniel.

6. What was the decree that these men persuaded the king to make? _____
    _____
    _____

7. What did Daniel continue doing? _____
    _____

8. How did Darius show his faith in the true God? [6:16]
    _____
    _____
    _____

9. How do we know that Daniel spent the night in the den of lions? _____
    _____

10. That night the king could not _____ or _____.

11. God's _____ had shut the mouths of the lions.

12. What happened to his enemies? _____
    _____
    _____

13. How was the earth filled again with the knowledge of
    the glory of God? _____
    _____

14. Daniel prospered in the reign of _____ and in the
    reign of _____. [6:28]

15. "The _____ of Daniel" are in Daniel 7 – 12.

16. These prophecies were revealed to Daniel during the
    reigns of _____ [Daniel 7:1 and 8:1],
    _____ the Mede [Daniel 9:1], and the Persian king
    _____. [Daniel 10:1]

17. Prophetic scriptures are highly _____ .

18. A **symbol** is a _____ for something else.

19. The *"wind"* in Daniel 7:2 refers to God's _____ .

20. What are three rules for interpreting symbols?
    (1) _____
    (2) _____
    (3) _____
    _____

21. The two major interpretations of prophecy are
    (1) _____ and
    (2) _____

Lesson 8

The Four Beasts
Daniel 7

In the first year of Belshazzar king of Babylon, Daniel had a dream and visions in his head upon his bed. **7:1** Belshazzar began his reign fourteen years before the fall of Babylon in 539 BC, making the date of the vision 553 BC.[43] This is the same Belshazzar who saw the hand that was writing on the wall in Daniel 5. The visions were different scenes that were all connected to one dream. He then wrote down what he had seen and heard.

Behold, the four winds of the heaven strove upon the great sea. **7:2** The *sea* symbolizes the ungodly nations. The *wind* represents the action of God. [See page 54.] The "great sea" may be referring to the Mediterranean Sea, as it is called by that name. All four kingdoms mentioned in Daniel 7 were connected to the Mediterranean Sea. The theme of Daniel is seen in this vision: *"The Most High rules in the kingdom of men."* [Daniel 4:17]

And four beasts came up from the sea. **7:3** They were different from each other. Verse 17 reveals that the four beasts are *"four kings which shall arise out of the earth."* They also represent the kingdoms of these four kings, because *"the fourth beast shall be the fourth kingdom,"* according to verse 23. In the book of Revelation, a beast came up from the sea having seven heads, which symbolized seven kings and their kingdoms. [Revelation 13:1-2; 17:10]

---

[43] Jim McGuiggan, *The Book of Daniel*, p. 107

The first beast was like a *lion* with wings of an eagle, symbolizing the **Babylonians. 7:4** Lions with wings guarded the gates of the palaces in Babylon. "They were practically emblems of the Babylonian power." [44] Jeremiah compared Babylon to a lion, and Ezekiel called the king of Babylon a great eagle. [45] The lion being stripped of his wings describes the humbling of Nebuchadnezzar in Daniel four when he lost his throne while living in the fields like an animal. The lion being made to stand on two feet like a man and being given the heart of a man symbolize the restoration of his throne and his understanding. Even before God drove Nebuchadnezzar from his throne to live among the animals, he had been behaving like a beast in his cruelty and pride. After God showed him his true condition, he became a man who humbly acknowledged and praised *"the Most High"* who is *"the King of heaven."* [Daniel 4:34, 37] This tells us what it means to be "a man" in God's sight.

A *bear* symbolized the next kingdom, the empire of the **Medes & Persians. 7:5** The bear was raised up on one of its sides predicting that the Persians would be the dominant power. The *"three ribs"* in its mouth reveal that this kingdom would be three times (or many times) larger than the kingdom of Babylon and would grow in three directions—*"westward, and northward, and southward."* [8:4, 20] The bear was commanded, **"Arise, devour much flesh."**

A *leopard* represented Alexander the Great and the kingdom of the **Greeks. 7:6** The swift leopard with four

---

[44] Paul T. Butler, *Daniel*, p. 260
[45] Jeremiah 50:17; Ezekiel 17:3, 12

wings represents the speed with which Alexander would conquer the world. The *"four heads"* represent the four kingdoms into which the empire was divided eventually.

The fourth kingdom is represented by ***a dreadful and strong beast with ten horns and great iron teeth.*** **7:7** The crushing power of the **Romans** is described by this terrifying beast that was very strong like iron. In Daniel 2, the iron in the legs and feet of the great statue represents the Romans, who came after the Greeks.

These four beasts symbolize the same four kingdoms that are represented by the great statue in Daniel 2. The Babylonians are the lion and the statue's head of gold. The Medes & Persians are the bear and the statue's chest and arms of silver. The Greeks are the leopard and the statue's belly and thighs of bronze. And the Romans are the dreadful beast with ten horns and iron teeth and the statue's legs of iron and feet of iron and clay.

As Daniel was thinking about the ten horns of the fourth beast, ***there came up among them another little horn.*** **7:8** In addition to the ten horns there was *"another"* horn, an eleventh horn. Before this little horn, ***there were three of the first horns plucked up by the roots.*** **7:8** Thus the little horn became the eighth horn. This little horn had ***eyes like the eyes of a man and a mouth that was speaking pompous words.*** **7:8** NKJV The meaning of the symbolism of these horns is revealed by an angel in verses 15-28.

Daniel continued to look until thrones were set in place, and ***the Ancient of Days did sit.*** **7:9** "The Ancient of Days" is God the Father in heaven. The purity of

God's nature is suggested by his clothing being as *"white as snow"* and his hair like *"pure wool."* God's justice and judgments are symbolized by his throne being like a *"fiery flame"* and by *"the books"* that were opened. This is not the final Day of Judgment because Christ the Son will be the judge on that day. [Acts 17:31] The *"wheels"* on God's throne may indicate the speed of his judgments or perhaps the wheels of a war chariot indicating his wrath. God has the power to execute his judgments because he has thousands upon thousands to serve him and ten thousand times ten thousand standing by to carry out his will. **7:10**

The boastful words of the little horn held Daniel's attention. He kept looking at the fourth beast until it was killed and destroyed with fire. **7:11** This describes the fall of the Roman Empire along with the humanism of the other beasts that had lived on in the Romans. **7:12** In the dream of Nebuchadnezzar, the rock smote and destroyed the statue that represented these four kingdoms. [2:32-35, 44-45]

The Vision of the Kingdom of Christ
Daniel 7:13-14

"I saw in the night visions, and behold, one like the Son of Man came with the clouds of heaven, and came to the Ancient of Days." **7:13** The Son of Man refers to Christ. This is the first time that these words are used to describe the Christ. Jesus referred to himself as "the Son of Man" more than seventy times. For example, Jesus said, *"The Son of Man came not to be ministered unto, but to minister, and to give his life a ransom for many."* [Matthew 20:28] Others like Ezekiel were called

"son of man" to emphasize their humanity. The divine Son of God was also the Son of Man in his humanity.

When Christ completed his redemptive work on earth, he ascended through the clouds into heaven. [Acts 1:9] It is important that we have the right perspective of this vision; it is from heaven's point of view. Daniel saw Christ coming from the earth through the clouds and approaching God the Father on his throne in heaven. He was brought into the Father's presence.

And there was given him dominion, and glory, and a kingdom. **7:14**   After his resurrection, Jesus declared, *"All power (authority) is given unto me in heaven and in earth."* [Matthew 28:18] On the day of Pentecost, Peter proclaimed that Jesus is by the right hand of God exalted, having received of the Father the promise of the Holy Spirit that he would sit on David's throne. [Acts 2:33, 30]

All people, nations and languages should serve him: his dominion is an everlasting dominion, which shall not pass away, and his kingdom that which shall never be destroyed. **7:14.** The kingdom of Christ covers the entire earth and includes those of all people and nations. This is the kingdom that is predicted in Daniel 2:44; it is the one that shall stand forever. The kingdom of Christ shall replace the kingdoms represented by the four beasts.

Those that have been redeemed by the blood of Christ are now in the kingdom of Christ. The heavenly Father *"has delivered us from the power of darkness and has translated us into the kingdom of his dear Son: in whom we have redemption through his blood, even the forgiveness of sins."* [Colossians 1:13-14] Christ's spiritual kingdom is his church. [Matthew 16:16-19] The kingdom of God came with power on the day of Pentecost following the death, burial, and resurrection of Jesus in fulfillment of Daniel's prophecies. [Read: Mark 1:14-15, Mark 9:1, Luke 24:46-49, Acts 1:1-8, and Acts 2:1-47.]

The Vision of the Four Beasts Explained
Daniel 7:15-28

The writer plainly identifies himself as "Daniel" who saw visions that "troubled" him during the first year of Belshazzar king of Babylon [verse 1]. **7:15** He could not understand the vision of the four beasts and the other visions that were related to it. He saw God judging from his throne in heaven. He saw the beast with the ten horns slain. He saw the Son of Man coming to God and receiving a kingdom. Daniel did not know how all these scenes were connected. So he asked an angel to explain the meaning of all that he had seen. **7:16**

"The four beasts are four kingdoms that will rise from the earth." **7:17** ^{NIV} They are the Babylonians, the Medes & Persians, the Greeks, and the Romans. These kingdoms come from the ungodly nations of the earth, which are symbolized by the sea. [7:3]

The vision of the Son of Man coming before the Ancient of Days was explained in this way: *"But the saints of the Most High will receive the kingdom and will possess it forever."* **7:18** ^{NIV} The impressive kingdoms of the world will rise and fall, but God has something better for his saints. In the days of the Roman kingdom, Christ would be given an eternal kingdom for God's people to enjoy. Persecutions by the

Jews and by the Romans would not destroy it, but the saints will have God's kingdom forever. Paul reminds Christians that *"our light affliction, which is but for a moment, is working for us a far more exceeding and eternal weight of glory."* [2 Corinthians 4:17]

Daniel wanted to know more about the fourth beast with the ten horns and the little horn. **7:19, 20 *This horn was waging war against the saints and defeating them.* 7:21** NIV The angel gave the following explanation.

"The fourth beast shall be the fourth kingdom upon the earth." **7:23** The Roman Empire was the fourth kingdom. *"And the ten horns out of this kingdom are ten kings that shall arise; and another shall arise after them, and he shall be diverse from the first, and he shall subdue three kings."* **7:24** The ten horns are the first ten Roman emperors. Premillennialists insist that the ten horns are ten modern European nations ruling at the same time. But the angel said they are "ten kings" from "the fourth kingdom", the Roman kingdom. The eleventh Roman emperor is *"another horn, a little one."* [7:8, NIV] This "little horn" is a king that would come "after" the first ten kings, suggesting that the other kings came after each other.

The First Eleven Roman Emperors

1. Augustus, 27 BC to 14 – Christ's birth, Luke 2:1
2. Tiberius, 14 to 37 – Christ's ministry, Luke 3:1
3. Caligula, 37-41
4. Claudius, 41-54
5. Nero, 54-68

6. Galba, 68 to 69, ruled a few months, then killed*

7. Otho, 69, ruled only a short time, then murdered*

8. Vitellius, 69, ruled just briefly, then murdered*

9. **Vespasian, 69-79, father of Titus and Domitian**

10. **Titus, 79-81**

11. **Domitian, 81-96, "the little horn"**

* The three kings uprooted (killed) before "the little horn" were Galba, Otho, and Vitellius. The eighth king to establish his throne was Domitian.

Domitian is "the little horn" of the fourth kingdom *"before whom there were three of the first horns plucked up by the roots."* [7:8] Galba, Otho, and Vitellius were murdered before Domitian came to power. The eleventh king *"shall subdue three kings."* [7:24] Vespasian was the father of Domitian. F. F. Bruce says, "Vespasian was hailed as 'restorer of the world' because of his great services in mending the disjointed state after the civil strife that followed Nero's death." [46] Domitian subdued these three kings in the same way that Levi paid tithes through Abraham. [Hebrews 7:9] If Levi could pay tithes through his ancestor Abraham, surely Domitian could be said to subdue these three kings through his father Vespasian.

All of the other things said about the "little horn" accurately describe Domitian. In the "little horn" were *"eyes like the eyes of man."* Domitian was very suspicious and had many spies, symbolized by these "eyes" in verse 8.

[46] F. F. Bruce, *The Spreading Flame*, p. 162

The "little horn" speaks great arrogant words against God. [7:8, 25] Domitian was presumptuous and unbridled in actions and words and demanded that he be addressed as "Our Master and Our God." [47] He wanted to be worshiped.

In Daniel's vision, the "little horn" was making war against the saints; he was oppressing and defeating them." [7:21, 25] In the book of Revelation, when the beast *"makes war"* he is persecuting God's people. Domitian was the persecutor at the time Revelation was being written. The early church historian Eusebius wrote, "With terrible cruelty, Domitian...showed himself Nero's successor in hostility to God. He was the second to organize a persecution against us, though his father Vespasian had no such evil plans." [48]

And the saints will be handed over to him for a time, times and half a time. 7:25 [NIV] In Revelation 11:7-11, the beast comes up out of the bottomless pit and makes war against the two witnesses, and the saints are dead for three-and-a-half days. This symbolizes a short period of persecution. Domitian was the first Roman emperor to accuse Christians of "treason" if they did not worship him. Nero had persecuted the saints for personal reasons—as a scapegoat for the fire of Rome. After Domitian, there would be ten more Roman emperors that would persecute Christians as "traitors" to the empire. [Rev. 17:12-14] The "little horn" embodied the spirit of the beast that lived on after Domitian's death in AD 96.

---

[47] Suetonius, *Lives of the Twelve Caesars* (Suetonius, a Roman historian)
[48] Paul L. Maier, *Eusebius—The Church History*, p. 107

The premillennialists ignore these plain facts of history and declare that the "little horn" of Daniel 7 is the Antichrist, a future world ruler. The Antichrist has already come. [1 John 2:18-22]

After the fall of the Roman Empire, the spirit of the fourth beast lives on in other humanistic governments. In the book of Revelation, a beast having seven heads and ten horns is a composite of the four beasts that are in Daniel 7. The beast blasphemes God and persecutes his people. [Rev. 13:1-8] *"But the judgment shall sit, and they shall take away his dominion, to consume and to destroy it unto the end."* **7:26** This beast was *"cast alive into a lake of fire burning with brimstone."* [Rev. 19:20] This is the final judgment!

Daniel 7:27 is looking forward to the sounding of the seventh trumpet in Revelation 11:15, *"The kingdom of the world has become the kingdom of our Lord and of his Christ, and he will reign for ever and ever."* NIV The saints of the Most High will inherit this kingdom in heaven. They will enter *"into the everlasting kingdom of our Lord and Savior Jesus Christ."* [2 Peter 1:11]

There are two purposes for the vision in Daniel 7. *First,* the vision of the four beasts shows that Christ would establish his kingdom during the time of the Roman Empire. *Second,* it shows that Christ's kingdom will never be destroyed—even persecution will not destroy it.

Review Questions on Lesson 8

1. "The _____ _____" is the vision of Daniel 7.

2. Daniel had a dream in the first year of _____ king of Babylon.

3. Four Beasts came up out of the _____.

4. A _____ represents the Babylonians.

5. A _____ represents the Medes & Persians.

6. A _____ represents Alexander and the Greeks.

7. A beast with _____ _____ represents the Romans.

8. The fourth beast also had huge teeth of _____.

9. These four beasts represent the same _____ as the statue in Nebuchadnezzar's dream in Daniel 2.

10. The ten horns of the fourth beast represent the first ten _____ of the Roman Empire.

11. The first Roman emperor _____ was king at the time of Christ's _____.

12. The second Roman emperor _____ was king during Christ's _____.

13. A _____ horn came up after the first ten horns.

14. Three of the first horns were _____.

15. The eleventh Roman emperor was _____, the little horn.

16. The little horn spoke arrogant words against whom? [7: 25]

    _____

17. The little horn would _____
    the saints.

18. Who were the "three uprooted horns" -- kings that ruled
    only for a short time and then were murdered?
    _____, _____,
    and _____.

19. Who was the father of Domitian? _____

20. Domitian's _____ were symbolized by
    the little horn's eyes.

21. Domitian demanded to be addressed as "Our _____
    and our _____."

22. The early church historian Eusebius wrote that the
    successor of Nero in the persecution of Christians was

    _____.

23. The two purposes of the vision in Daniel 7 are to show:
    (1) that Christ and his kingdom would come in the time
        of the _____ Empire and
    (2) that Christ's kingdom will never be _____.

Lesson 9

The Ram and the Goat
Daniel 8

This chapter gives a closer view of two kingdoms that were described in chapter seven.

In the third year of the reign of King Belshazzar a vision appeared unto me, even unto me Daniel. **8:1** The date was about 550 BC. The writer again identifies himself as Daniel, who lived at that time.

In this vision, Daniel saw himself in the city of Susa, also called Shushan, in the Persian province of Elam. He was by the River Ulai, which was near the city. **8:2** Later, the story of Esther takes place in this city during the time of Ahasuerus, whom the Greeks called Xerxes (485 to 465 BC).

Daniel saw *a ram with two horns* standing by the River Ulai. *And the two horns were high, but one was higher than the other, and the higher came up last.* **8:3** The explanation of the ram is given in verse 20. The two horns of the ram are the kings of Media and Persia. At first, the kings of Media were dominant; but beginning with Cyrus the kingdom became known as the Persian Empire. Compare these two horns of the ram with the bear that was raised up on one side in Daniel 7:5.

Daniel saw *the ram pushing westward, and northward, and southward.* **8:4** The kingdom of the Medes and Persians was east of Babylon. And like a strong ram, it pushed westward and conquered the Babylonian Empire of the Chaldeans. Next, it charged to the north and then to the west until it reached Greece. It

also advanced to the south to include all of Egypt,
Libya, and Cyrenaica. The ram did according to his will,
and became great. This kingdom became known as the
great Persian Empire that was much larger than any
kingdom before it.

As Daniel was thinking about the ram, suddenly he
saw *a male goat with a great horn* between his eyes
coming from the west and crossing the surface of the
whole earth without touching the ground. **8:5** According
to verse 21, the goat represents the kingdom of Greece,
and the great horn is the first king. Alexander the Great
was the first king of the Greek Empire. A horn is a
symbol for a king. Greece is west of Persia, so the goat
came from the west. His going across the surface of the
earth without touching the ground symbolizes the extent
and speed of Alexander's conquests.

Then Daniel saw the goat coming toward the ram.
The goat confronted the ram and charged at him with
great rage breaking the ram's two horns. The ram was
powerless against the goat, so the goat trampled him into
the ground. **8:6, 7** Alexander and the Greeks defeated
the Persians in the year 330 BC. According to the first
century Jewish historian Josephus, when Alexander
came to Jerusalem in 332 BC, he was shown this
prophecy in Daniel 8. He recognized that he was the
goat in the prophecy and responded by treating the Jews
with kindness.[49] Alexander's empire became very great.
8:8 It included Egypt, Libya, and Cyrenaica in Africa
and extended to the Indus Valley in India. Alexander

---

[49] Flavius Josephus, *Antiquities*, XI, viii, 5

wanted to continue his conquests, but in 326 BC his men refused to go any farther. They returned to the Persian city of Persepolis in 324 BC. "In a short span of 13 years, without losing a single battle, Alexander had acquired the largest empire the world had ever seen." [50]

Therefore the male goat waxed very great: and when he was strong, the great horn was broken. **8:8** Alexander died in the city of Babylon in 323 BC at the age of 33. He was only 20 years old when his father, Philip II king of Macedonia, was assassinated. After gaining the support of the army, he became king and began his conquests. As a youth, Alexander had been trained for three years in the Greek culture by Aristotle. In his conquests, Alexander spread the use of the Greek language throughout the world. God was preparing the world for the gospel of Christ that would be revealed in the New Testament, written in Greek. Christ also died at age 33, but instead of losing a kingdom, he received a kingdom. [7:14]

After the great horn of the goat was broken off, four horns came up in its place. **8:8** The explanation is given in verse 22, that four kingdoms will come out of that nation. After Alexander died, his kingdom was eventually divided into four kingdoms, *"but not in his power."* These four kingdoms were ruled by four men who had been in Alexander's army. Cassander ruled over Macedonia and Greece. The kingdom of Lysimachus was Asia Minor and Thrace. Ptolemy was king of Egypt. Seleucus founded the Seleucid dynasty in Syria in 312 BC and built Antioch as

[50] Stearns, Schwartz, Beyer, *World History*, p. 99, Addison-Wesley

his capital city. His kingdom included Syria, Babylon, and Persia, but it later expanded to include Cilicia and Asia Minor.[51]

Out of one of the four horns came *"a little horn"* that grew great in power toward the south, toward the east, and toward the land of Palestine, called the pleasant, beautiful, and glorious land. **8:9** This little horn was Antiochus IV, the eighth king of the Seleucid dynasty, and he reigned from 175 to 164 BC. He extended his power to the south (Egypt), to the east (Persia), and to Palestine, the Holy Land.

A coin of Antiochus IV has his image on one side and on the reverse side a figure of Jupiter, the chief god of the Romans, with the inscription in Greek that is translated: "Of King Antiochus, God Illustrious, victorious." He claimed to be the incarnation of Jupiter, and he called himself "Theos Epiphanes" meaning "God Illustrious" [52] or "God Manifest." [53]

Like the Roman emperor Domitian, Antiochus IV was *the eighth* king of his kingdom, and like Domitian, he demanded to be worshiped as a god. The power of God is symbolized by the number eight. The LORD's covenant with Abraham required every male child to be circumcised on "the eighth day" to have God's blessing. God's power was demonstrated when Jesus was raised from the dead on the first day of the week, which was called also "the eighth day" by early Christians as in the Epistle of Barnabas.[54]

---

[51] Edward M. Burns, *Western Civilizations*, p. 158
[52] *McClintock-Strong Cyclopedia of Biblical...*, "Antiochus IV," p. 272
[53] *Encyclopedia Britannica*, "Antiochus IV"
[54] *Encyclopedia Biblica*, III (1902), "Lord's Day," p. 2815

The little horn grew until it reached the host of the heavens, and it threw some of the starry host down to the earth and trampled on them. **8:10** ^{NIV} The descendants of Abraham are compared with the stars of heaven in Genesis 15:5. The interpretation is given in verse 24, *He shall destroy the mighty men and the holy people.* Antiochus IV replaced Onias the high priest with his brother Jason, who was willing to promote the Greek culture, including idolatry.[55] In a three-day period, Antiochus IV killed 80,000 Jews, including women and children.[56] In the following days, many other Jews suffered horrible deaths rather than abandon their faith in God. [57] Daniel 8:25 had predicted that this king *"shall destroy many."*

The little horn set itself up to be as great as the Prince of the host. **8:11** ^{NIV} The Prince of the host is the God of Israel. Antiochus IV tried to destroy the worship of the true God, and he desecrated his holy temple in Jerusalem. He took away the daily sacrifice and offered unclean swine upon the holy altar. The LORD's temple was made a place of idolatry. He erected an altar to the god of drunkenness, and all kinds of immoralities were committed there.

Many unfaithful Jews were eager to adopt the ways of the Greeks and they aided Antiochus in his fight against the LORD. Because of them, truth was cast down to the ground. **8:12** He attempted to destroy the Holy Scriptures.

---

[55] 2 Maccabees 4:7-20
[56] 2 Maccabees 5:11-14
[57] 2 Maccabees 6:6-7:4

If God's people do not love and appreciate the truth, they will lose it. Before the nation of Israel was carried away by the Assyrians, God gave them this warning: *"Behold, the days come, says the Lord GOD, that I will send a famine in the land, not a famine of bread, nor a thirst for water, but of hearing the words of the LORD."* [Amos 8:11]

An angel informed Daniel that the persecution against the faithful Jews and the desecration of the temple would last *"unto two thousand and three hundred days; then shall the sanctuary be cleansed."* **8:13-14** "The number 2300 has no symbolic significance, as some numbers in prophecy have. Apparently, therefore, it is a literal period of time. 2300 days is a little less than 6½ years. It is also the amount of time which elapsed from the time Antiochus deposed the legitimate high priest, Onias, until the temple was finally cleansed." [58] Onias was removed from his office and killed in 171 BC, and the temple was rededicated on December 25, 165 BC. [59]

Judas Maccabeus and his small army of Jews defeated the large forces of Antiochus and regained the temple and cleansed it. This victory is celebrated today by the Jews with the feast of **Hanukkah**, which means *dedication.* [John 10:22] The feast lasts for eight days with the lighting of one candle each day until eight candles are burning to commemorate the miraculous oil in the lampstand (menorah) that continued to provide light for

[58] John A Copeland, *A Study of Daniel*, p. 43, Quality Publications
[59] Albert Barnes, *Barnes Notes* on Daniel 8:14

eight days in 165 BC. Hanukkah is also called the Feast of Lights.

After seeing the vision of the ram and the goat, Daniel was seeking to understand its meaning. The angel Gabriel came to Daniel and explained the vision. **8:15-17** He said to Daniel, *"Look, I am making known to you what shall happen in the latter time of the indignation; for at the appointed time the end shall be."* **8:19** ^{NKJV} He was speaking about the persecution of the Jews by Antiochus IV and how it would end. Unfaithful Jews would bring severe suffering upon their nation. *"When rebels have become completely wicked, a stern-faced king, a master of intrigue, will arise. He will become very strong, but not by his own power."* **8:23** ^{NIV} "God was going to use him to punish the wicked among the Jews." [60] Antiochus would be lifted up in pride as he used craftiness and deceit. *"Yet he will be destroyed, but not by human power."* **8:25** ^{NIV}. God would destroy him—not man. God struck him with an incurable disease of the intestines, and he died a very painful and disgusting death in 164 BC.

The death of Antiochus IV is described in 2 Maccabees 9:4-9. "Transported with rage, he conceived the idea of turning upon the Jews the injury done by those who put him to flight; so he ordered his charioteer to drive without stopping until he completed his journey. But the judgment of heaven rode with him! For in his arrogance he said, 'When I get there, I will make Jerusalem a cemetery of the Jews.' But the all-seeing Lord, the God

---

[60] John A. Copeland, *A Study of Daniel*, p. 44

of Israel, struck him with an incurable and unseen blow. As soon as he ceased speaking he was seized with pain in his bowels for which there was no relief and with sharp internal tortures ... Yet he did not in any way stop his insolence, but was even more filled with arrogance, breathing fire in his rage against the Jews, and giving orders to hasten the journey. And so it came about that he fell out of his chariot as it was rushing along, and the fall was so hard as to torture every limb in his body. Thus he who had just been thinking he could command the waves of the sea, in his superhuman arrogance ... was brought down to earth and carried in a litter, making the power of God manifest to all. And so the ungodly man's body swarmed with worms, and while he was still living in anguish and pain, his flesh rotted away, and because of the stench the whole army felt revulsion at his decay." [RSV] [61]

Daniel was instructed to *"seal up the vision, for it concerns the distant future."* 8:26 NIV The prophecy of the "little horn" would be fulfilled over three hundred years after Daniel had seen the vision. The command to "seal up the vision" was to keep it safe and to preserve it so that when it was fulfilled in 171 to 164 BC, the people would know that the LORD had predicted these events. [cf. Isaiah 8:16-17]

The vision was so upsetting to Daniel that it made him sick for several days, but he got up and returned to work for Belshazzar king of Babylon. 8:27

[61] First and Second Maccabees are uninspired books of the Apocrypha; however they relate the history between the Old and New Testaments.

Review Questions on Lesson 9

1. When was the vision of "The Ram and the Goat"?
   _____

2. Daniel saw himself in the city of _____ in Elam.

3. Who interpreted the vision for Daniel? _____

4. The ram's two horns represent the kings of _____
   and _____.

5. Who was the "higher" horn of the ram? _____

6. The goat symbolizes the kingdom of _____.

7. Who was the great horn of the goat? _____

8. The goat came from what direction? _____

9. The breaking of the ram's two horns and being
   trampled by the goat is predicting the _____ of
   the Medes & Persians by the Greeks in _____ BC.

10. When the goat's one great horn was broken off, this
    was a symbol of the _____ of Alexander at age
    _____.

11. The four horns that grew up in the place of the broken
    horn represent four _____ that would
    come out of that nation.

12. Who became the king of Syria and Babylon and built
    the city of Antioch in Syria for his capital? _____

13. Who began a long line of kings in Egypt? _____

14. Antiochus IV is symbolized by a _____ _____
    that came from one of the four horns.

15. Antiochus IV called himself *"Theos Epiphanes"* which means "_____ _____."

16. The power of _____ is symbolized by the number "8."

17. Why was Onias the high priest removed in 171 BC?

    _____

18. Antiochus took away the daily _____ and made God's temple a place of _____ .

19. He "cast _____ to the ground" by trying to destroy the Holy _____. [8:12]

20. What was the reason for this severe persecution and the desecration of God's temple? _____

    _____

21. When was the temple cleansed and rededicated to the Lord? _____

22. Who defeated the army of Antiochus and regained the temple for the LORD? _____

23. What feast do the Jews still celebrate today that is a commemoration of this event? _____

24. How did Antiochus IV die? _____

    _____

Lesson 10

A Prayer for God's People
Daniel 9:1-21

More than eleven years had passed since the vision of "The Ram and the Goat" in chapter eight. Babylon had fallen to the Medes and Persians. Darius the Mede had become king over the realm of the Chaldeans, the former kingdom of Babylon. In the first year of this king, Daniel prayed, making humble supplications on behalf of God's people in exile. **9:1** The year was 538 BC.

As he read the Holy Scriptures, Daniel understood by the word of the LORD that came to Jeremiah the prophet that the desolations of Jerusalem would last seventy years. **9:2** There were two desolations: one of the people and the other of the land. The captivity of the people would last seventy years, according to Jeremiah 29:10-14. Daniel knew that the seventy years would be completed soon—within two years. The first captives, including Daniel, were taken to Babylon in 606 BC, and the Jews were allowed to return to Jerusalem in 536 BC. The captivity of the people lasted seventy years. Jeremiah also wrote, *"And this whole land shall be a desolation."* [Jer. 25:11] The temple and the city of Jerusalem were destroyed in 586 BC, and the rebuilding of the temple was completed in 516 BC—"seventy years" later.

Daniel set his face toward Jerusalem to pray to God with fasting, dressed in sackcloth and covered with ashes. **9:3** [cf. 6:10] When Solomon dedicated the temple in Jerusalem, he mentioned in his prayer the possibility of God's people being taken captive to a foreign land because of their sins. Solomon asked God to hear in heaven and forgive his people when they return to him with all their heart in the land of their enemies and pray toward Jerusalem and the temple. [1 Kings 8:48-50] God had promised, *"After seventy years are accomplished at Babylon, I will visit you and perform my good word toward you, in causing you to return to this place. ... Then shall you call upon me, and you shall go and pray unto me, and I will hearken unto you. And you shall seek me and find me, when you shall search for me with all your heart."* [Jeremiah 29:10, 12-13] This is why Daniel was so earnest in prayer that he did not eat. He wore sackcloth and ashes as signs of repentance and mourning. His prayer is one of the great prayers of the Bible.

Daniel began his prayer with praise, **"O Lord, the great and awesome God, who keeps his covenant of love with all who love him and obey his commands."** **9:4** ^{NIV} Praise to God preceded his requests. With reverential fear, Daniel acknowledged God's greatness and his faithfulness to his covenant of mercy with those who love him and keep his commandments. *"The effectual fervent prayer of a righteous man avails much."* [James 5:16]

After praising God, Daniel went directly to the source of their suffering. He plainly confessed, **"We have sinned and have committed iniquity."** **9:5** Included in the meaning of the word **iniquity** is the failure to measure up to what is required. Although Daniel had been devoted to the LORD from his youth [1:8] and was "greatly beloved" by God [9:23], he recognized his own sins and imperfections when he said, "**We** have sinned." He did not say, "**They** have sinned" or "Nebuchadnezzar sinned against us." Instead of self-righteously blaming others, Daniel identified himself with his people in their sins. They had been wicked and had rebelled by not obeying God's commandments and laws. They had not listened to the prophets who had preached to them, warning them of the consequences of their sins. **9:5, 6**

Daniel contrasted God's holiness with the sins of his people: *"Lord, you are righteous, but this day we are covered with shame."* **9:7** ^{NIV} Judah and all Israel had been scattered among other countries because of their unfaithfulness to God. Their sins were more than violations of the law; they were personal offenses against God. Daniel confessed, *"We have sinned against you."* **9:8**

Another contrast is God's mercy and man's rebellion. *"To the Lord our God belong mercies and forgiveness, though we have rebelled against him."* **9:9** They did not deserve forgiveness. They needed mercy. *"Neither have we obeyed the voice of the LORD our God, to walk in his laws, which he had set before us by his servants the prophets."* **9:10** Daniel is praying to God, but he is speaking of God in the third person: "him" and "he." Do not criticize a brother today if he does the same thing in his public prayers. It is scriptural! He is still talking to God. A husband may say to his wife after eating her cooking, "My wife is a great cook!"

"Therefore the curse is poured upon us, and the oath that is written in the Law of Moses the servant of God, because we have sinned against him." **9:11** They were suffering because of their sins. They had been warned in Leviticus 26:14-35 and Deuteronomy 28:15-64 that if they did not obey the LORD they would be scattered

among the nations and their land would be desolate and their cities destroyed. Daniel recognized Moses as the writer of the Pentateuch. The Law of Moses was still binding and valid although it had been given hundreds of years earlier. The new covenant of Christ is still true and effective today although many years have passed by. We are warned: *"Therefore we must give the more earnest heed to the things we have heard, lest we drift away. For if the word spoken through angels proved steadfast, and every transgression and disobedience received a just reward, how shall we escape if we neglect so great a salvation, which at the first began to be spoken by the Lord, and was confirmed to us by those who heard him."* [Hebrews 2:1-2, NKJV]

Daniel acknowledged God's trustworthiness in his prayer. ***"He has confirmed his words, which he spoke against us and against our judges who judged us, by bringing upon us a great evil. For under the whole heaven has not been done as has been done upon Jerusalem. As it is written in the Law of Moses, all this evil has come upon us; yet made we not our prayer before the Lord our God, that we might turn from our iniquities, and understand your truth." 9:12-13*** A great calamity is called an "evil". Besides prayer, they needed to turn away from their sins in repentance and give attention to God's truth, his word. We have the same need today. Prayer alone is not enough. Also notice that it is scriptural to make reference to God's word in our prayers. We may pray, "As it is written in Acts 2:38..."

Daniel returned to addressing God in the first person. ***"And now, O Lord our God, who has brought your*** *people forth out of the land of Egypt with a mighty hand, and has gotten you renown, as it is this day; we have sinned, we have done wickedly."* **9:15** We need to remember how God has blessed us in the past. He has saved us from our sins and has delivered us from hardships and difficulties. God is merciful and powerful. Notice the number of times Daniel confesses their sins.

Daniel prayed that the Lord's anger and wrath would be turned away from his city Jerusalem. He acknowledged that Jerusalem and God's people had become a reproach among the nations because of their sins. **9:16** So Daniel prayed, *"Now therefore, O our God, hear the prayer of your servant, and his supplications, and cause your face to shine upon your sanctuary that is desolate, for the Lord's sake."* **9:17** Daniel is humbly and earnestly requesting for God to be glorified in the restoration of Jerusalem.

"O my God, incline your ear and hear." **9:18** God's exalted position in heaven is high above man. As a father would bend down to hear his little child, Daniel is asking God to hear the prayers of his people.

"Open your eyes and see the desolation of the city that bears your Name. We do not make requests of you because we are righteous, but because of your great mercy." **9:18** ᴺᴵⱽ Jerusalem remaining in ruins was reflecting poorly upon God's greatness and glory. Daniel's appeal to God is not based upon the righteousness of his people, because they have brought ridicule and shame upon the city. He desires mercy. He prays for the restoration of Jerusalem so that God's righteousness and power may be made known to all.

Daniel concludes his prayer with short, simple petitions that spring from a heart that desires to honor God. *"O Lord, listen! O Lord, forgive! O Lord, hear and act! For your sake, O my God, do not delay, because your city and your people bear your Name."* **9:19** NIV

While Daniel was praying, confessing his sins and the sins of his people, the angel Gabriel came to him. **9:20-21** The angel appeared in the form of a man, just as the LORD and two angels appeared to Abraham in Genesis 18:2 – 19:1. He was the angel who had explained the vision of the ram and the goat in Daniel 8:15-16. Gabriel also was the angel who was sent to the virgin Mary hundreds of years later to tell her about the birth of Christ and his eternal kingdom. [Luke 1:16-33] It is fitting for the angel Gabriel to be the one who would tell Daniel about the prophecy that would be fulfilled in Christ.

Review Questions on Lesson 10

1. The events of chapter nine were in the _____ year of the reign of _____ the Mede in _____ BC.

2. Daniel understood the prophecy made by _____ the prophet.

3. The desolations of Jerusalem would last _____ years.

4. The first captives were taken in _____ BC.

5. The exiles were allowed to return in _____ BC.

6. The captivity of the people lasted _____ years.

7. The temple was destroyed in _____ BC.

8. The temple was restored in _____ BC.

9. The temple was in desolation for _____ years.

10. What well known event in Daniel's life occurred about the same time of his prayer in Daniel 9:3-19? [Daniel 6] _____

11. Daniel was in the habit of praying toward what city? [6:10] _____

12. Daniel was so earnest in prayer that he did not _____.

13. He wore sackcloth as a sign of _____.

14. Daniel began his prayer with _____.

15. God keeps his _____ with all who love him and _____ his commands. [9:4]

16. Daniel's confession was "We have _____
    and committed _____."

17. They failed to hear God's servants the _____.

18. "Lord, you are _____, but
    this day we are covered with _____."
    [9:7, NIV]

19. The curse and the oath of sworn judgments were
    written in the _____ of _____.
    [9:11]

20. Their sin was a personal offense against _____.

21. Besides prayer, God's people must turn away from their
    sins in _____.

22. Daniel remembered how God brought his people out of
    the land of _____, where they had been
    slaves.

23. What had caused Jerusalem to be made a reproach to
    the nations around them? _____

24. Daniel concludes his prayer with short petitions,
    saying: "O Lord, _____!" "O Lord, _____!"
    "O Lord, _____ and _____!" "For
    _____ sake, O my God, do not _____,
    because your _____ and your _____
    bear your _____." [9:19, NIV]

25. The angel _____ came to Daniel
    while he was still in prayer confessing sins.

Lesson 11

The Seventy Weeks
Daniel 9:20-27

While Daniel was praying, the angel Gabriel came to give him understanding about the future of his people. Daniel was given the vision of the seventy weeks, because he was "greatly beloved" and "highly esteemed". His prayer was answered as soon as he began to pray. **9:20-23**

Gabriel said that **"seventy weeks"** had been decreed for Daniel's people, the Jews, and for his holy city, Jerusalem. **9:24** Seven is a perfect number, and ten is a complete number. Seven times ten is seventy. In seventy weeks, God's purpose for the Jews and for their city of Jerusalem would be completely fulfilled. God had chosen Abraham, Isaac, and Jacob and their descendants to bring into the world the promised Seed, the Christ, who would bless all nations and families.[62]

Every commentary I've read agrees that the weeks are not the usual weeks of days, but weeks of years — 490 years. However, some take the 490 years to be literal years, while others say they are figurative. In Daniel 8:14, we took the 2,300 days to be literal days because it fit the length of time from the removal of Onias the high priest to the cleansing of the temple. Also, that number had no symbolic significance for the period that was being described. We will see that a literal 490 years does not fit the period being described by the seventy weeks. But all the numbers used in the vision of the seventy weeks have symbolic meaning.

---

[62] Genesis 22:15-18, Genesis 26:1-5, Genesis 28:10-14, Galatians 3:16

Why 490 years? Every seventh year a Sabbath rest for the land was to be observed according to the law in Leviticus 25:1-4. The Jews were captives in Babylon *"until the land had enjoyed her Sabbaths. . . to fulfill the seventy years."* [2 Chron. 36:20-21] From the time of the Judges to the Babylonian exile, it appears that God's people had failed to observe the Sabbaths for the land more than seventy times. The "seventy years" are symbolic for all the Sabbaths they had failed to observe.[63] Since the land Sabbath came every seventh year, this would be a period of 490 years (70 x 7).

As Daniel anticipates the completion of the seventy years and the return of the Jews to Jerusalem, Gabriel tells him of another symbolic 490 years. Jim McGuiggan says, "When these 'seventy weeks' have 'run their course' God will have finished *altogether* his work with the Jews as a (Mosaic) commonwealth!" [64]

Seventy weeks are determined . . . to finish the transgression, to make an end of sins, to make reconciliation for iniquity, to bring in everlasting righteousness, to seal up vision and prophesy, and to anoint the Most Holy." 9:24   Christ fulfills this prophecy.

First, **The transgression is finished.** Sin entered the world because of the transgression of Adam, but through the righteous act of Christ, his atoning sacrifice, many will be justified. [Romans 5:12-19]

---

[63] Leviticus 26:27-35
[64] Jim McGuiggan, *The Book of Daniel*, p. 151

Second, **An end of sins has been made.** *"We are sanctified through the offering of the body of Jesus Christ once for all."* [Hebrews 10:10] *"And their sins and iniquities I will remember no more."* [Hebrews 10:17]

Third, **Reconciliation for iniquity has been made.** *"God was in Christ, reconciling the world to himself, not imputing their trespasses to them, and has committed to us the word of reconciliation."* [2 Corinthians 5:19]

Fourth, **Everlasting righteousness** has been brought in. The apostle Paul wrote that he wanted to be found in Christ, *"not having mine own righteousness, which is of the law, but that which is through the faith of Christ, the righteousness which is of God by faith."* *"For I am not ashamed of the gospel of Christ, for it is the power of God unto salvation to everyone that believes...for therein is the righteousness of God is revealed."* [Philippians 3:9; Romans 1:16-17]

Fifth, **Vision and prophesy have been sealed up.** God *"has in these last days spoken unto us by his Son."* [Hebrews 1:1-2] *"How shall we escape, if we neglect so great salvation, which at the first began to be spoken by the Lord and was confirmed unto us by them that heard him?"* [Hebrews 2:3] Jesus said to his apostles, *"But the Comforter, which is the Holy Spirit, whom the Father will send in my name, he shall teach you **all things**. He will guide you into **all truth**."* [John 14:26; 16:13] Peter stated, *"His divine power has given to us **all things** that pertain unto life and godliness."* [2 Peter 1:3] Jude exhorted, *"Contend earnestly for the faith which was once for all delivered to the saints."* [Jude 3, NKJV]

Paul wrote, *"If anyone preaches any other gospel to you than what you have received, let him be accursed."* [Galatians 1:9, NKJV] *"Love never fails. But where there are prophesies, they will cease."* [1 Cor. 13:8, NIV] That's sealing up vision and prophecy.

Sixth, **The Most Holy Place in heaven has been anointed.** *"Christ came as High Priest. . . . With his own blood He entered the Most Holy Place once for all, having obtained eternal redemption. . . For Christ has not entered the holy places made with hands...but into heaven itself."* [Hebrews 9:11, 12, 24, NKJV] After Jesus died on the cross, he entered into heaven, and with his own blood he made atonement for sins and sealed the New Testament, the final revelation of God to man. That's anointing the Most Holy.

The angel Gabriel explained to Daniel, **"Know therefore and understand that from the going forth of the command to restore and build Jerusalem unto the Messiah the Prince shall be seven weeks and sixty-two weeks."** 9:25

The command or the decree to rebuild Jerusalem was made by Cyrus king of Persia. Isaiah had predicted this over one hundred and fifty years earlier. *"Thus says the LORD, your redeemer ... who says of Cyrus, 'He is my shepherd, and shall perform all my pleasure, even saying to Jerusalem, 'You shall be built,' and to the temple, 'Your foundation shall be laid.'"* [Isaiah 44:24, 28] Most likely this prophecy was the means by which God *"stirred up the spirit of Cyrus"* to make the following proclamation: *"Thus says Cyrus king of Persia, The LORD God of heaven has given me all the kingdoms of the earth; and he has charged me to build him a house at Jerusalem, which is in Judah. Who is there among you of all his people? His God be with him, and let him go up to Jerusalem, which is in Judah, and build the house of the LORD God of Israel, he is the God which is in Jerusalem."* [Ezra 1:1-3]

The proclamation of Cyrus is obviously the decree to rebuild Jerusalem. The command to build the city came before the command to build the temple in Isaiah 44:28. The Jews upon their return to Jerusalem spent the first year building the city. [Ezra 3:8-13] In fact, they got so busy building houses for themselves they left off building God's house. The LORD sent his prophet Haggai to encourage them to finish building the temple. [Haggai 1:2-4, 7-9]

From the return of the Jews to rebuild Jerusalem until the coming of Jesus Christ, the Messiah, there would be seven weeks plus sixty-two weeks, making a total of sixty-nine weeks or 483 years. If these years are taken literally the prophecy seems to miss the birth of Christ by 53 years, because the decree of Cyrus was in 536 BC. Therefore, these years must be symbolic.

The "seventy weeks" are divided into three periods: seven weeks, sixty-two weeks, and the seventieth week.

During **the first seven weeks,** or 49 years (7 x 7), the temple and the wall of Jerusalem would be built again, *even in troublesome times.* 9:25 "Adversaries" troubled the Jews in their building the temple and caused the work to cease for a while. [Ezra 4] And years later, there were enemies who made trouble for those who were rebuilding the wall. [Nehemiah 4] The time from the decree of Cyrus in 536 BC to the completion of the walls by Nehemiah in 445 BC was a period of over 90 years, not 49 years. This is further proof that these "weeks" must be symbolic. Seven is a perfect and complete number. Seven times seven means that God would completely restore the temple and Jerusalem during this period.

The **"sixty-two weeks"** represent the period from the completion of the Old Testament to the coming of Christ, the Messiah. Sixty-two in itself is not a symbolic number, but multiply 62 times 7 and you get 434. "Four" is the symbolic number for the world, and "three" represents the Godhead. During this period between the writing of the Old Testament and the New Testament there were no inspired writers or prophets. However, this was the period of 4-3-4. God (3) was in the middle of the world (4) working in a providential way. In the second century BC, God was working in the world in the time of Antiochus IV as we have already seen in Daniel 8. The number 434, God in the world, perfectly describes the time between the Testaments.

The **seventieth week**, the last seven years of the 490 years, represents the first century when Christ came to finish the transgression, to make an end of sins, to make reconciliation for iniquity, to bring in everlasting righteousness, to seal up vision and prophecy, and to anoint the Most Holy. [9:24] Gabriel's prophecy was *"that from the going forth of the commandment to restore and to build Jerusalem unto Messiah the Prince shall be seven weeks and sixty-two weeks."* [9:25]

Christ would come after a total of sixty-nine weeks or 483 years. What is the significance of 4-8-3? Read the numbers from right to left, and you have God (3) was in Christ (8) reconciling the world (4). 2 Corinthians 5:19 reads, *"God was in Christ, reconciling the world unto himself."* Early Christians used the number "8" for Christ, since he was raised from the dead on the first day of the week, which is also the "eighth" – the day after the seventh. The number "8" represents God's power. [Daniel 8:9, page 71] Jesus was *"declared to be the Son of God with power...by the resurrection from the dead."* [Romans 1:4] Both the Greek king Antiochus IV and the Roman king Domitian were the eighth rulers of their kingdoms, and they claimed to be a god in the flesh. Jesus Christ was the only true incarnation of divinity. He is the one mediator between the world and God [1 Tim. 2:5-6]. The world (4) – Christ (8) – God (3).

You should be able to see that every one of the numbers in the "seventy weeks" has a symbolic meaning that describes the period that it represents.

Gabriel predicted **the death of Christ** during the first century: *"**And after sixty-two weeks shall Messiah be cut off, but not for himself.**"* **9:26** He will die for others. He tasted death for everyone. [Hebrews 2:9] His death was the means of making reconciliation and everlasting righteousness possible. *"God demonstrates His own love for us, in that while we were still sinners, Christ died for us."* [Romans 5:8. NKJV]

Gabriel also predicted the destruction of Jerusalem in the first century: ***"And the people of the prince that shall come shall destroy the city and the sanctuary; and the*** *end thereof shall be with a flood, and unto the end of the war desolations are determined."* **9:26** The prince was Titus, the son of Vespasian, the Roman emperor. He led his army against Jerusalem and destroyed the city and the temple in AD 70. Jesus had predicted this. He said, *"O Jerusalem, Jerusalem...how often would I have gathered your children together, even as a hen gathers her chickens under her wings, and you would not! Behold, your house is left unto you desolate."* [Matthew 23:37-38] In Matthew 24, Jesus described the destruction of the temple and Jerusalem, and he concluded in verse 34 that it would be in the first century. This destruction marked the end of God's use of Jerusalem and the temple. "Seventy weeks" had been determined for "the holy city."

And he shall confirm the covenant for one week. **9:27** The antecedent of "he" is the Messiah in verse 26. The "one week" is the "seventieth week." In the new covenant of Christ, Jerusalem is no longer the center of worship. Worship is in a spiritual place. During his ministry, Jesus said the hour was coming *"when the true worshipers shall worship the Father in spirit and in truth."* [John 4:20-23]

During the first century Christ made and confirmed the new covenant. Hebrews 9:15 states: *"He is the mediator of the new testament, that by means of death, for the redemption of the transgressions that were under the first testament, they which are called might receive the promise of eternal inheritance."* This covenant of salvation *"was confirmed unto us by them that heard him; God also bearing them witness, both with signs and wonders."* [Hebrews 2:3, 4] Christ confirmed the new covenant with his blood. When he instituted the Lord's Supper, he said, *"For this is my blood of the new testament, which is shed for many for the remission of sins."* [Matthew 26:28] His apostles and other inspired writers in the first century confirmed the covenant with various miracles and the completion of the New Testament. [Mark 16:17-20, 2 Peter 1:3] At the end of the seventieth week, vision and prophecy were to cease.

***But in the middle of the week, He shall bring an end to sacrifice and offerings.* 9:27** ᴺᴷᴶⱽ After Jesus' ministry of three-and-a-half years,[65] he brought an end to sacrifice and offerings by the sacrifice of himself on the cross. Christ, *"after he had offered one sacrifice for sins forever, sat down on the right hand of God . . . For by one offering he has perfected forever them that are sanctified."* [Hebrews 10:12, 14] *"We are sanctified through the offering of the body of Jesus Christ once for all."* [Hebrews 10:10] There is no need for a temple in Jerusalem with its sacrifices and offerings under the old covenant. Christ has confirmed the new covenant with his one sufficient sacrifice.

***"And for the overspreading of abominations he shall make it desolate, even until the consummation."* 9:27** Jesus made reference to this prophecy and applied it to

---

[65] Richard Trench on John 5:1, "If this feast was a Passover, then John will make mention of four Passovers, namely, this one, and in John 2:13, 6:4, and the last. Thus, we shall arrive at **the three and one half years, the half of a week of years,** for the length of Christ's ministry, which many have thought they found designated beforehand for it in the prophecies (Daniel 9:27)." Those agreeing with this view include: Irenaeus (2ⁿᵈ century), Eusebius, Luther, Matthew Henry, Adam Clarke, J.W. McGarvey, Burton Coffman. Like the ministry of Christ, a period of 3.5 years symbolizes the evangelism of the church in Rev. 11:3-12.

the destruction of Jerusalem in AD 70. He said, *"When you therefore shall see* **the abomination of desolation, spoken of by Daniel the prophet,** *stand in the holy place...then let them which are in Judea flee to the mountains...Verily I say unto you, this generation shall not pass till all these things are fulfilled."* [Matt. 24:15, 16, 34] Luke 21:20 tells us that Jesus also said, *"When you see Jerusalem being surrounded by armies, you will know that its desolation is near."* [NIV]

The abominations of the Jews would cause the desolation of the city of Jerusalem. As the Roman armies advanced from the north and west toward the city, a crafty Jewish zealot named John with his band of outlaws escaped from Galilee to Jerusalem.[66] Upon entering the city, they encouraged the young men to join them in their resistance to the Romans. Their numbers grew until these ruthless men gained control of the city and "came into the sanctuary with polluted feet." They made the temple of God their stronghold, and the sanctuary became a "refuge and a shop of tyranny." These zealots deposed the rightful high priest and made an unworthy "rustic" man the high priest.[67] Flavius Josephus, the Jewish historian, was an eyewitness of these events and recorded them in his writings.[68]

Christians in Jerusalem saw these "abominations" in the temple and the Roman armies closing in on the city and they fled to a city of Perea called Pella.[69] They

[66] Flavius Josephus, *Wars of the Jews*, Book IV, Chapter II
[67] Flavius Josephus, *Wars of the Jews*, Book IV, Chapter III, Sections 1-8
[68] *International Standard Bible Encyclopaedia*, "Josephus, Flavius"
[69] Paul L. Maier, *Eusebius – The Church History*, Section 3.5, p. 95

escaped the horrors that were to come, because they heeded the warning!

Even before the Romans came to Jerusalem, there was terrible bloodshed in the city. Gorian the son of Josephus and Symeon the son of Gamaliel assembled a large force to fight against the zealots and "to purge the temple of these polluters" who had slaughtered their own countrymen. So the two groups fought each other, "and great slaughter was made on both sides." [70] When the zealots invited the Idumeans to come to their aid, there were 12,000 of the nobility who were brutally put to death.[71] With the Jews fighting each other, the Romans came up and besieged the city.

Predicting the "desolation" of Jerusalem, Jesus said, *"For then shall be great tribulation, such as was not since the beginning of the world to this time, no, nor ever shall be. And except those days should be shortened, there should no flesh be saved."* [Matthew 24:21-22] Josephus estimated that 1.1 million died by famine and the sword.[72] For the terrible sufferings in Jerusalem during the siege, read *Wars of the Jews*, Book VI, by Josephus. "Seventy weeks" had been determined for Daniel's holy city of Jerusalem.

Coffman concluded, "Jesus Christ himself related this vision to the destruction of Jerusalem by the Romans; that settles it." [73] The "seventy weeks" ended with the

---

[70] Josephus, *Wars of the Jews*, Book IV, Chapter III, Sections 9-12

[71] Josephus, *Wars of the Jews*, Book IV, Chapters IV – V, Sections 1-3

[72] Maier, *Eusebius – The Church History*, Section 3.7, page 101,
  Quoting Josephus, *Wars of the Jews*, Book VI, Chapter IX, Section 3

[73] Burton Coffman, *Coffman's Bible Commentary*, Daniel 9:20-27

destruction of Jerusalem in AD 70. Not before; not later. You have Christ's word for it!

God's purpose for the nation of Israel was to bring the Christ into the world. Jerusalem and the temple served as types and shadows of the heavenly things. Having completed their purpose, their religious significance has come to an end. Jesus Christ has brought to us a new covenant with everlasting righteousness. This is the message of the vision of "the seventy weeks".

Those who take a literal view of the "seventy weeks" are divided into two groups: the premillennialists and the non-premillennialists.

The non-premillennialists start with Artaxerxes' decree in 458 BC that authorized Ezra to lead the second group of exiles back to Jerusalem. [Ezra 7:11-17] By adding the 483 years of the 69 weeks to this date you come to AD 25. The ministry of Jesus began when he was 30 years old, and if you adjust for the error in our calendar the date would be AD 25. Jesus was born in 5 BC. Our calendar is off by five years. The ministry of Jesus was three-and-a-half years, which would place his death "in the middle of the week," the last seven years. This interpretation sounds good at first.

However, this theory does not match the years at the beginning and the end of the seventy weeks. The first seven weeks, or 49 years, were for restoring Jerusalem. [9:25] The city was completely restored by 444 BC with the rebuilding of the walls by Nehemiah. Instead of 49 years for rebuilding the city, it would be only 14 years. Malachi had completed the Old Testament by 425 BC—

only 33 years later. This interpretation does not fit! In the seventieth week, the temple was not destroyed three-and-a-half years after Jesus' death. The temple was destroyed in AD 70; Jesus was crucified no later than AD 33. This interpretation misses the destruction of Jerusalem by over 30 years. That's not even close.

The premillennialists start with the date in 445 BC, when king Artaxerxes wrote letters for Nehemiah to rebuild the walls of Jerusalem. [Nehemiah 2:1-9] They admit that from this decree to Christ's ministry, this interpretation misses it by over 13 years (470 instead of the 483), but they say that is close enough.[74] They also miss the first seven weeks. The walls were completed within a year of the decree to rebuild them—not 49 years! That's not even close! In fact, the walls were rebuilt in 52 days during Nehemiah's first year in Jerusalem. [Nehemiah 6:15]

Both literal views begin with the wrong decree. The decree to rebuild Jerusalem was given by Cyrus in 536 BC. Surely, when Daniel heard this decree, he thought his prayer was answered! For God had said through his prophet Isaiah, *"Thus says the* LORD *to his anointed, to* **Cyrus,** *... 'He shall build my city and he shall let go my captives.'"* [Isaiah 45:1, 13] That should settle the question of when the command was given "to restore and build Jerusalem." [9:25]

For an interpretation to be true, **all** the facts must agree. If the prophecy of the "seventy weeks" is to be interpreted literally all the facts must agree. But as we

[74] Robert D. Culver, *The Wycliffe Bible Commentary*, p. 794

have seen, they do not. However, if the numbers are taken to be symbolic, they **all** have meaning and accurately describe the time they represent. If any of the numbers had failed to do this, we would have rejected this approach. But none of them do. They all agree! The "seventy weeks" are symbolic.

Under the topic "Number", *Fausset's Bible Dictionary* makes the following statement: "Daniel and Revelation use several numbers to characterize periods, rather than indicate arithmetical duration."

Review Questions on Lesson 11

1. "Seventy weeks" were determined for Daniel's people, the _____, and for his holy city, _____.

2. The "weeks" are not weeks of days, but of _____.

3. Every 7th year was to be a Sabbath for the _____.

4. While the Jews were in Babylon the land enjoyed her _____, according to 2 Chronicles 36:21.

5. The 70 years of captivity was in payment for the ____ years in which the land Sabbath was not observed.

6. The angel _____ tells Daniel of another symbolic 490 years, the "seventy weeks."

7. Seventy weeks were determined...
   (1) to finish the _____,
   (2) to make an end of _____,
   (3) to make _____ for iniquity,
   (4) to bring in everlasting _____,
   (5) to seal up _____ and _____, and
   (6) to _____ the Most Holy (Place). [9:24]

8. How are the "seventy weeks" divided? [9:25]
   _____

9. The "seventy weeks" begin with the command to restore and rebuild what city? [9:25] _____

10. God said of _____ that he would say to Jerusalem, "You shall be built." [Isaiah 44:24, 28]

11. During the first seven weeks, the city and the walls were to be _____, "even in _____ times."

12. What is the symbolic meaning of the first seven weeks or 7 x 7? _____
   _____

13. The sixty-two weeks represent the period between the _____ _____ and _____ _____.

14. What is the symbolic meaning of 4-3-4 (62 x 7)?
   _____
   _____

15. Who was to come after 69 weeks, 483 years?
   _____

16. What symbolic meaning can be given to 4-8-3?
   _____
   _____

17. What is the meaning that "Messiah shall be cut off, but not for Himself"? _____

18. Messiah will confirm a _____ for one week.

19. In the middle of the seventieth week, Christ shall bring an end to _____ and _____.

20. The destruction of the city of _____ in AD 70 is predicted in the "seventy weeks" prophecy.

21. Who said that Daniel's prophecy of "the abomination of desolation" would be fulfilled in the first century?
   _____

Lesson 12

The Latter Days of the Jews
Part 1
Daniel 10:1 – 11:35

A prophecy concerning the latter days of the Jews was revealed to Daniel in 534 BC, the third year of Cyrus king of Persia. **10:1** It was about an appointed time that involved a long war between the kings of Syria to the North of Judah and the kings of Egypt to the South. The Jews were caught in the middle of this great struggle that is described in detail beginning with Daniel 11:5. This rivalry intensified in the time of Antiochus IV. In Daniel 8:9-25, we were introduced to this wicked ruler who called himself *Theos Epiphanes*, "God Illustrious". He would bring an extended persecution against the Jews and would desecrate God's temple, but the Jews would be victorious in the end.

As he wrote about this vision, Daniel explained how he felt at that time. *"In those days I, Daniel, was mourning three full weeks."* **10:2** Daniel was mourning for three **weeks of days**. This was a period of twenty-one days, according to verses 12 and 13. This emphasis proves that in the previous chapter the seventy weeks were figurative **weeks of years**. Daniel now is using literal language.

The Jews were allowed to return to Jerusalem in the first year of Cyrus in 536 BC. [Ezra 1:1-6] The foundation of the temple in Jerusalem had been laid in 535 BC, but the work of rebuilding had ceased. [Ezra 3:8 and 4:1-5]

Without the temple, the feasts days could not be observed properly. Daniel's three weeks of mourning ended on the twenty-fourth day of the first month. **10:4** The Passover feast was from the fourteenth day to the twenty-first day of the first month. [Exodus 12:1-15] The opposition to the building of the temple at this time explains Daniel's sadness.

Daniel was on the bank of the Tigris River when he saw a great angel of God. **10:4-9** His appearance was similar to that of Christ in Revelation 1:13-16. Angels reflect the glory of God. In Revelation 10:1, a mighty angel appeared to be like both God the Father and the Son. Although only Daniel saw the vision, the men who were with him were filled with terror and hid themselves. Daniel was alone when he saw the vision of the great angel. He lost his physical strength and felt helpless. As the angel spoke to him, he fell into a deep sleep with his face to the ground.

Then a hand touched Daniel that caused him to tremble on his hands and knees. **10:10** The angel said to him, *"O Daniel, a man greatly beloved, understand the words that I speak unto you, and stand upright: for unto you am I now sent."* When he said this, Daniel stood up trembling. **10:11** Then the angel said, *"Fear not, Daniel: for from the first day that you did set your heart to understand and to chasten yourself before my God, your words were heard."* **10:12** God heard his prayer when he first began to pray, but the answer was delayed for three weeks. The answers to our prayers also may be a long time in coming. Paul Butler says, "What a consolation to know that God hears those of humble and contrite hearts—hears and is able to answer. When a man's attitude arrives at the attitude Daniel had, God is more than willing to act on that man's behalf to that man's ultimate good. Such a man may not always understand the answer God gives or the method God uses to answer, but such a man will accept it in faith and trust." [75]

The angel explained why he was delayed in coming to Daniel. ***"But the prince of the kingdom of Persia withstood me twenty-one days: but, lo, Michael, one of the chief princes, came to help me; and I remained there with the kings of Persia."*** **10:13** Michael is called "the archangel" in Jude 9 and "your prince" in Daniel 10:21. Speaking of those who believe in him, Jesus said, *"...their angels always see the face of my Father who is in heaven."* [Matthew 18:10] Angels, both good and evil, are called "princes" in Daniel 10:13. "The prince of the kingdom of Persia" seems to be a demonic angel that was fighting against the Lord's angel that was sent to Daniel. We are informed in Ephesians 6:12 that *"we wrestle not against flesh and blood, but against principalities, against powers, against the rulers of the darkness of this world, and against spiritual wickedness in the high places."* Although God "rules in the kingdom of men," Satan also has some influence over kingdoms and gives power to wicked rulers. [Revelation 13:2] But in the end, God is sovereign and victorious!

The angel explained his mission. ***"Now I have come to make you understand what will happen to your people in the latter days, for the vision refers to many days yet to come."*** **10:14** NKJV This is the theme of the

---

[75] Paul T. Butler, *Daniel*, p. 378

last three chapters—the latter days of the Jews. Zechariah spoke of the days before the exile in Babylon as "the former days"— making the days after the exile "the latter days." [Zechariah 8:7-11] The angel is not speaking of the last days before the end of time. He is revealing the last days of the Mosaic Dispensation. God's special working through the Jews as a nation came to an end during the first century with the coming of Christ and the Holy Spirit and the establishment of the church. The destruction of Jerusalem and the temple in AD 70 showed the removal of God's favor from physical Israel.

Daniel bowed his face and was speechless. When the angel touched his lips, Daniel was able to speak, and he said, *"I have retained no strength...neither is there breath left in me."* The angel touched Daniel again and strengthened him. And the angel said, *"O man greatly beloved, fear not: peace be unto you, be strong, yes, be strong."* And Daniel was strengthened. **10:15-19**

The angel asked, *"Do you know why I have come to you?"* **10:20** NIV Butler says, "The angel's question is rhetorical. Daniel should remember that the angel had been sent to overcome the evil-angel who was being allowed to influence the decisions and actions of the rulers of Persia. God's angel had overcome this evil-spirit and now announces that he is about to return and continue such overruling. Evidently God's angelic helper to Persia will not go unchallenged, but he will have to continue the spiritual struggle (in the realm of the unseen spiritual world) just so long as God deems it necessary to fulfill His work with the covenant people preparing them to bring forth the Messiah." [76] This angel's providential working through Esther saved the Jewish nation from being destroyed.

The angel then spoke of the future. *"And when I go, the prince of Greece will come."* **10:20** [NIV] Butler says, "As soon as the one conflict ends with Persia, the angel will be engaged in the same sort of conflict with another demonic-angel sent from hell to attempt to thwart God's plans by influencing the rulers of Greece. If God's angel were not there, demon influence might well meet with success...The same God is alive today and He can, if He wishes, and will, if necessary, provide a great host of heavenly beings to minister to those who inherit salvation [cf. Heb. 1:14; 2 Kings 6:14-19]." [77]

The angel promised Daniel, *"I will show you that which is noted in the scripture of truth."* **10:21** The following prophecies are given in such amazing accuracy and details that their truthfulness cannot be denied. In fact, the liberal critical scholars declare that it must be history. After Daniel had interpreted Nebuchadnezzar's dream, he concluded, *"And the dream is certain, and the interpretation thereof is sure."* [2:45; cf. Rom. 4:17] Daniel accurately predicted the future kingdoms, including the Medes & Persians, the Greeks, the Romans, and God's eternal kingdom. God's prophetic word is indeed "the scripture of truth."

Michael the archangel was the only one that helped the angel speaking to Daniel in his fight against Satan's

---

[76] Paul T. Butler, *Daniel*, p. 385
[77] Paul T. Butler, *Daniel*, p. 385

angels. **10:21** Darius the Mede had been confirmed as king and given strength by God's angel. **11:1** The theme of the book of Daniel is *"The Most High rules in the kingdom of men, and gives it to whomsoever he will."* [Daniel 4:17]

The Future of the Jews[78]
Daniel 11:2-35

Behold, three more kings will arise in Persia, and the fourth shall be far richer than them all; by his strength, through his riches, he shall stir up all against the realm of Greece. **11:2** [NKJV] The three kings in Persia that followed Cyrus were **Cambyses** (his son), **Pseudo-Smerdis** (a pretender who usurped the throne for seven months), and **Darius I**, also called Hystaspis. In the reign of Darius, the temple in Jerusalem was completed with the aid of his decree. [Ezra 6] The fourth king was **Xerxes,** who is called Ahasuerus in the book of Esther. His great power and wealth are described in Esther 1:1-7. Both Darius and Xerxes were defeated in attempts to conquer the Greeks. After the death of Xerxes in 465 BC, the power of Persia began to decline although there were seven more kings.

And a mighty king shall stand up, that shall rule with great dominion, and do according to his will. **11:3** Alexander the Great with his army of Greeks conquered the entire Persian Empire by 327 BC without losing a single battle and went on to rule over the largest empire the world had ever known.

---

[78] Paul T. Butler, *Daniel.* pp. 407-463, gives the historical events that fulfill the prophecies in Daniel 11 and 12.

His kingdom shall be broken up, and shall be divided toward the four winds . . . and not to his posterity. **11:4**   When Alexander died in 323 BC at a young age, his great empire was divided into four kingdoms, because he did not have an heir to his throne.

The king of the South will become strong, but one of his commanders will become even stronger than he and will rule his own kingdom with great power. **11:5** ^NIV Ptolemy I, called Soter, was "the king of the South" in Egypt. In 301 BC, Seleucus, who was one of Ptolemy's generals, joined with Lysimachus and Cassander in defeating Antigonus, who was claiming the empire of Alexander. Due to this victory, Seleucus became independent of Ptolemy and ruled over the largest of the four divisions of the Greek empire. He founded the city of Antioch in Syria as his capital.

After some years, they will become allies.   The daughter of the king of the South will go to the king of the North to make an alliance, but she will not retain her power, and he and his power will not last. In those days, she will be handed over, together with her royal escort and her father and the one who supported her. **11:6** ^NIV   In an attempt to end the wars between them, Antiochus II "the king of the North" married Bernice, the daughter of Ptolemy II, in 252 BC. Antiochus II was already married to Laodice but separated from her. When Ptolemy II died in 250 BC, Antiochus II divorced Bernice and took back Laodice as his wife. But Laodice had Antiochus poisoned and Bernice and her infant son murdered to secure the throne for her son, who became Seleucus II in 246 BC.

But from a branch of her roots one shall arise in his place, who shall come with an army, enter the fortress of the king of the North, and deal with them and prevail. **11:7** ^{NKJV} In 245 BC, Bernice's brother (of her roots), Ptolemy III, invaded Syria in retaliation for her death and was successful in gaining much territory and putting Laodice to death. Then he was called back to Egypt to deal with a local problem. *For some years he will leave the king of the North alone.* **11:8** ^{NIV}

Then the king of the North will invade the realm of the king of the South but will retreat to his own country. **11:9** ^{NIV} In 240 BC, Seleucus II succeeded in regaining much of his lost territory, including Damascus. But when he tried to invade Egypt, he was defeated and had to return home. Peace was made that year, and Ptolemy III made no further attacks on Syria.

His sons will prepare for war and assemble a great army, which will sweep on like an irresistible flood and carry the battle as far as his fortress. Then the king of the South will march out in a rage and fight against the king of the North, who will raise a large army, but it will be defeated. **11:10-11** ^{NIV} The king of the North, Seleucus II, had two sons — Seleucus III and Antiochus III. The older son, Seleucus III (226-223 BC), died in battle in Asia Minor, and his brother was made king when he was only 18 years old. Antiochus III reigned from 223 to 187 BC, and became known as Antiochus the Great. By the spring of 217 BC, Antiochus had conquered all of Palestine and reached the border of Egypt. However, the army of Ptolemy IV defeated the large army of Antiochus III near the border town of Raphia.

And when he has taken away the multitude, his heart shall be lifted up; and he shall cast down many, ten thousands, but he shall not be strengthened by it. **11:12** The Syrians lost 10,000 infantry and 300 cavalry. Ptolemy IV resumed his life of luxury and died in 203 BC without strengthening his imperial fortifications.

For the king of the North will muster another army, larger than the first; and after several years, he will advance with a huge army fully equipped. **11:13** ^{NIV} Egypt was weakened after the death of Ptolemy IV, because his heir was only a child of four years. Antiochus III was able to regain all of Syria by the spring of 198 BC.

In those times many will rise against the king of the South. The violent men among your own people will rebel in fulfillment of the vision; but without success. **11:14** ^{NIV} Many allies helped Antiochus III when he invaded Egypt the second time, including some belligerent Jews. They thought this was the time to revolt against their Egyptian rulers and realize their dream of independence, but they were wrong. The future kings of the North would be even more exacting in their rule over them. *Then the king of the North will come and build siege ramps and will capture a fortified city. The forces of the South will be powerless to resist; even their best troops will not have the strength to stand. The invader will do as he pleases; no one will be able to stand against him. He will establish himself in the Beautiful Land and will have the power to destroy it.* **11:15, 16** ^{NIV} Antiochus III, also called Antiochus the Great, took control of Palestine, *the Beautiful Land*, including Jerusalem.

And he will set his face to come with the power of his whole kingdom, bringing with him a proposal of peace which he will put into effect; he will also give him the daughter of women to ruin it. But she will not take a stand for him or be on his side. **11:17** ^{NASB} Antiochus III came to Ptolemy V (204-181 BC) with a show of force and a peace treaty in 198 BC. He betrothed his daughter Cleopatra (not the famous one) to young Ptolemy, and the marriage was consummated five years later. He was hoping to gain an influence over the king of Egypt through his daughter, but she constantly sided with her husband against her father.

Then he will turn his face to the coastlands and capture many. But a commander will put a stop to his scorn against him; moreover, he will repay him for his scorn. **11:18** ^{NASB} Antiochus III made conquests along the coasts of Asia Minor in 197 BC, then in Thrace a year later. When his conquests took him into Greece in 192 BC, he was met with resistance from two Roman generals. Acilius Glabio defeated him at Thermopylae in 191 BC. The next year, Cornelius Scipio put an end to his arrogant aggressions at Magnesia, near Ephesus. This commander forced him to pay an enormous tribute and took his younger son, Antiochus Epiphanes, as a hostage to Rome to ensure the tax payment.

Then he shall turn his face toward the fort of his own land; but he shall stumble and fall, and not be found. **11:19** Having lost all of his holdings west and north of the Taurus Mountains, Antiochus III returned home seeking to replenish his treasury. In 187 BC, he marched against the revolting Armenians and was killed by the Elamites when he tried to rob their temple.

His successor will send out a tax collector to maintain the royal splendor. In a few years, however, he will be destroyed, yet not in anger or in battle. **11:20** NIV The new king of Syria was Seleucus IV (187-175 BC). He was an older brother of Antiochus IV. Rome was demanding an enormous annual tribute. Seleucus had to heavily tax his subject nations, including Judea. The new king sent a tax collector, Heliodorus, to take money from the temple in Jerusalem, but an act of God prevented it. [2 Maccabees 3] Soon after that, Seleucus was poisoned by Heliodorus.

And in his place shall arise a vile person, to whom they will not give the honor of royalty; but he shall come in peaceably, and seize the kingdom by intrigue. **11:21** NKJV Antiochus IV (175-164 BC) was a vile person. Epiphanes meaning "illustrious one" was a name he had given himself, but the Jews called him "Epimanes" meaning "madman". No longer a hostage in Rome, he seized the throne by flattery and intrigue. [Read Daniel 8:9-25 and comments on pages 84-88.]

Then an overwhelming army will be swept away before him; both it and a prince of the covenant will be destroyed. **11:22** NIV He was known for defeating great armies, and deposing the prince of the covenant, the high priest Onias III.

After coming to an agreement with him, he will act deceitfully, and with only a few people he will rise to power. When the richest provinces feel secure, he will invade them and will achieve what neither his father nor his forefathers did. He will distribute plunder, loot and wealth among his followers. **11:23-24** NIV He became strong with only a small number of people by making agreements and then working deceitfully. He was able to capture Memphis and northern Egypt, which his fathers had been unable to do. He made friends by sharing the spoils of victory with his troops and also with the people in the lands he had conquered.

He shall stir up his power and his courage against the king of the South with a great army. And the king of the South shall be stirred up to battle with a very great and mighty army; but he shall not stand, for they shall devise plans against him. Yes, those who eat of the portion of his delicacies shall destroy him; his army shall be swept away. **11:25-26** ^{NKJV} Antiochus IV defeated the mighty army of Ptolemy VI because of intrigue within the Egyptian court in 171 BC. Even while his army was fighting, Ptolemy's trusted courtiers, Eulaeus and Lenaeus, were betraying him in favor of his brother Ptolemy Physkon, who was in control of Alexandria.

And both these kings' hearts shall be to do mischief, and they shall speak lies at one table; but it shall not prosper, for yet the end shall be at the time appointed. **11:27** At the peace table after the war, both kings lied to each other. Antiochus pretended that he wanted to help Ptolemy VI regain Alexandria and the half of Egypt that was under the rule of his brother Physkon, and Ptolemy lied when he said he trusted him. This alliance failed because "the appointed time" of God for peace had not yet come.

Then shall he return into his land with great riches; and his heart shall be against the holy covenant, and he shall do exploits, and return to his own land. **11:28**

On his way back home to Syria with great wealth from the war, Antiochus IV stopped at Jerusalem in 171 BC. He deposed the high priest Onias III and replaced him with his brother, Jason, who was willing to promote the Greek culture.

At the appointed time he will return and come into the South, but this last time it will not turn out the way it did before. For ships from Kittim will come against him; therefore he will be disheartened, and will return and become enraged at the holy covenant and take action; so he will come back and show regard for those who forsake the holy covenant. **11:29-30** NASB The phrase "at the appointed time" refers to God's providential rule in the kingdom of men. Antiochus tried to invade Egypt again in 168 BC, but was unsuccessful. Ptolemy VI and his brother Physkon united in asking the Romans for protection. In response, the Romans sent ships from Kittim (Cyprus) to Egypt. As Antiochus was besieging the city of Alexandria, the head of the Roman embassy, Laenas, confronted him and drew a circle in the sand around the king of Syria. He told Antiochus that he must decide to withdraw or step out of his circle and fight the Romans. He agreed to leave Egypt. But Antiochus vented his rage on the city of Jerusalem with the help of apostate Jews, to whom he showed favor. At this time, he slaughtered over 80,000 Jews before returning home.

His armed forces will rise up to desecrate the temple fortress and will abolish the daily sacrifice. Then they will set up the abomination that causes desolation. **11:31** NIV In that same year, 168 BC, Antiochus IV desecrated the temple and stopped the daily sacrifices to

God. In his attempt to force the Jews to adopt the Greek culture, he sent Syrian emissaries to Judea, who set up an image of Jupiter in the temple. They also offered swine on the altar and regularly observed a drunken orgy in worship of Bacchus. Jews were put to death for practicing circumcision and for observing the Sabbath and Jewish feast days. [I Maccabees]

And such as do wickedly against the covenant shall he corrupt by flatteries. **11:32** Some Jews were eager to accept and promote the Greek ways, thinking they would prosper. However, those who knew the Lord resisted.

And those who have insight among the people will give understanding to many; yet they will fall by sword and by flame, by captivity and by plunder, for many days. Now when they fall, they will be granted a little help, and many will join with them in hypocrisy. And some of those who have insight will fall, in order to refine, purge, and make them pure, until the end time; because it is still to come at the appointed time. **11:33-35** NASB The faithful Jews tried to teach others the right way, but they were killed or suffered extreme punishment. But their examples served to inspire others who would bring deliverance "at the appointed time". This period of suffering brought about the purification of the nation of the Jews.

Most, if not all, scholars are in agreement that Antiochus IV is the king in verses 21-35. However, beginning with verse 36 there are differences in opinion. Some say Herod the Great is the king, and others believe that the king of the North is the Romans.

The premillennialists say that this king is the Antichrist which they believe will come just before Christ's second coming. In the next lesson, we will attempt to prove that verses 36-45 are still speaking about Antiochus IV.

Review Questions on Lesson 12

1. Daniel 10-12 is "The _____ _____ of the Jews."

2. This prophecy was in the _____ year of Cyrus king of Persia in the year _____ BC.

3. The Jews would be in the middle of a long war between the kings of _____ to the _____ of Judah and the kings of _____ to the _____ .

4. The Syrian king _____ would bring an extended persecution against the _____ .

5. What caused Daniel to mourn for three weeks? [10:2-4 and Ezra 4:1-24] _____

   _____

6. What Jewish feast was at this time? _____

7. "The prince of Persia" a _____ _____ that fought against the Lord's angel that was sent to Daniel.

8. The archangel that helped the angel sent to Daniel was _____, who is called "your _____."

9. The days before the Babylonian exile were called "the _____ days" making those days after the exile "the _____ days" of the Jews, which also were the last days of the _____ Dispensation.

10. Why had the angel come to Daniel? [10:14] _____

    _____

11. The fourth king after Cyrus would be _____ who is called _____ in the story of Esther.

12. When the Persians attempted to conquer the _____, they were defeated.

13. The "mighty king" of Daniel 11:3 was _____ ____ _____.

14. The Greek Empire was divided into _____ lesser kingdoms after Alexander's death in 323 BC.

15. In 301 BC _____, a former general of Ptolemy I, founded the city of_____ in Syria and made it the capital of his new Seleucid kingdom.

16. The Seleucid king that took control of Jerusalem in 198 BC was _____.

17. In 190 BC, a Roman general took the younger son of Antiochus III, _____ _____, as a hostage to Rome to ensure the payment of a tribute tax.

18. In 175 BC, Antiochus IV seized the throne by _____ and _____.

19. What was this king able to do that his fathers could not do? [11:23-24] _____

20. In 171 BC, Antiochus IV deposed Onias III, the _____ _____ at Jerusalem.

21. In 168 BC, Antiochus IV killed over 80,000 _____ and desecrated the _____ and stopped the daily _____ to God.

22. This time of suffering brought about the _____ of the nation of the Jews.

NOTES

Lesson 13

The Latter Days of the Jews
Part 2
Daniel 11:36 – 12:13

The Reign of Antiochus IV Summarized
Daniel 11:36-45

This section summarizes the reign of Antiochus IV, who called himself *Theos Epiphanes*. Daniel uses this pattern of writing throughout the book. Four kingdoms are introduced in chapter two, and more is said about these same four kingdoms in chapter seven. A further explanation of two of these kingdoms is given in chapter eight. Daniel first introduces Antiochus IV in chapter eight. He mentions him again in 11:21-35 and reviews his life in 11:36-45, giving more details. This section is not about a future Anti-Christ.

And the king shall do according to his will. **11:36** Paul Butler states, "The king is none other than Antiochus Epiphanes. It is contrary to all sound principle of contextual exegesis to suppose that in a continuous description, with no indication whatever of a change of subject, 'the king' of verse 36 should be a different king from the one whose doings are described in verses 21-35." [79]

And he shall exalt himself and magnify himself above every god. **11:36.** On his coins, Antiochus IV called himself *Theos* (God) *Epiphanes* (Illustrious), the incarnation of Jupiter, the chief Roman god. [See comments, pages 84 -88] *The king shall speak ... against*

---

[79] Paul T. Butler, *Daniel*, p. 434

the God of gods, and shall prosper till the indignation is accomplished. **11:36** Antiochus IV plundered and desecrated the LORD's temple in Jerusalem, and he blasphemed God's holy name in word and deed. Because of *"the transgressors"* among the Jews, God was punishing and purifying his people with the wrath of Antiochus IV. The angel Gabriel said that the indignation (*"the time of wrath"*, NIV) would be during the time of the four Greek kingdoms, when a fierce king would persecute *"the holy people."* [Daniel 8:19-25] This king was not the Romans or some future Antichrist. Let the book of Daniel be its own interpreter. The king that is being described was Antiochus IV.

Neither shall he regard the god of his fathers, nor the desire of women, nor regard any god, for he shall magnify himself above all. But in his estate shall he honor a god whom his fathers knew not. **11:37, 38** Antiochus did not have regard for his national Greek god, Zeus, nor the Syrian deity, Tammuz-Adonis, "the desire of women." Instead, he honored Jupiter, a god that his fathers did not know, by erecting a temple to this supreme god of the Romans in his capital city of Antioch and adorning it with gold and silver and precious stones.[80] He learned about Jupiter while a hostage in Rome. As a means of controlling his subjects, he forced them, including the Jews, to worship his foreign gods.

A summary of the wars of Antiochus Epiphanes is given in verses **40-43**. Butler says, "This recapitulation of the overwhelming and devastating decade of Antiochus's reign would also make the prophecy [verses 44-45] of his end more emphatic."[81]

[80] F. W. Farrar, *The Book of Daniel* (The Expositor's Bible), p. 313
[81] Paul T. Butler, *Daniel*, p. 439

But reports from the east and the north will alarm him, and he will set out in rage to destroy and annihilate many. **11:44** [NIV] Antiochus had his armies in Judea trying to put down the revolt led by Judas Maccabeus when he got news from the east and the north that insurrection was spreading in Parthia and Armenia. Antiochus set out on a mission to put down these uprisings, leaving Lysias, one of his generals, behind with orders to destroy the Jews. However, God would destroy Antiochus before he could return to his home. In 165 BC, Lysias was defeated, and Judas Maccabeus regained possession of Jerusalem and cleansed the temple of its idolatry. This was followed by an eight-day feast called Hanukkah, the Feast of Dedication [John 10:22], or the Festival of Lights.[82] Antiochus himself suffered defeats in Persia.[83]

He will pitch his royal tents between the seas at the beautiful holy mountain. Yet he will come to his end, and no one will help him. **11:45** [NIV] Although for a time, Antiochus would spread his royal dominion over Jerusalem and Judea, between the Mediterranean Sea and the Dead Sea, yet he would die at the hand of the LORD. Daniel 8:25 speaks of Antiochus in a similar way, *"He will even oppose the Prince of princes; but he will be broken without human agency."* [NASB] Earlier, the *Glorious Land, the Beautiful Land,* is a reference to the Holy Land in Daniel 8:9. Here the *glorious, beautiful, holy mountain* is Mount Zion. [Psalm 48:2] This verse is not predicting where Antiochus would die, but how he would die. God would cause him to die a painful and humiliating death, and no one would help him. [Read 2 Maccabees 9:1-12]. Antiochus died at Tabae on the border of Persia and Babylon.[84]

---

[82] Paul T. Butler, *Daniel*, p. 439

[83] 2 Maccabees 9:1

[84] J. E. H. Tomson, *The Pulpit Commentary,* Vol. 13, Daniel, p. 325, and F.W. Farrar, *The Book of Daniel,* p. 317 (The Expositor's Bible)

The Victory of the Jews
Daniel 12

In chapter twelve, the angel is still explaining the future of Daniel's people, the Jews. He is promising them victory in the second century BC and their ultimate victory in Christ. When this angel first appeared to Daniel, he explained his mission. He said, *"Now I am come to make you understand what shall befall your people in the latter days."* [10:14] He is speaking of their last days as a favored nation under the old covenant. This is the same period as the seventy weeks that were to be for the Jews and for Jerusalem. [9:24] It is from the return to Jerusalem in 536 BC to the coming of Christ and the destruction of Jerusalem in AD 70. [9:25-27] This is the purpose of the prophecy in chapters ten through twelve. Then to make sure that Daniel would remember it, he asked in 10:20, *"Do you know why I have come to you?"* Do you understand? We also need to understand the purpose of this prophecy. It was to reveal the latter days of the Jews as a favored nation. This time frame must be remembered.

And at that time shall Michael stand up, the great prince which stands for the children of your people; and there shall be a time of trouble, such as never was since there was a nation even to that same time; and at that time your people shall be delivered, everyone that shall be found written in the book. 12:1. "And at that time" refers to the death of Antiochus IV, just mentioned in the previous verse. Michael, the great angel, would give support to the faithful Jews in a time of great trouble. This deliverance began with Judas Maccabeus and continued to the coming of the Messiah. Again, we can see the providential working of God during the period between the Testaments: 4-3-4. The Maccabees continued their difficult war against the Syrian armies before gaining independence for the Jews in 142 BC. The land of the Jews was free from foreign occupancy for seventy-nine years, although the kings of the south and the kings of the north continued to exist. [85]

The Jews lost their freedom in 63 BC, when the Roman general Pompey invaded the land. The fourth kingdom of Daniel's prophecy would be the Romans. [2:40] During this time, the kingdom of God would be established by Christ. [2:44, 7:23-27, 9:24-25] God would protect the Jews as a nation through troublesome times until his kingdom was established in the first century. Daniel 12:1 says, *"And there shall be a time of trouble, such as never was since there was a nation."* NKJV In Matthew 24:21, Jesus predicted the destruction of Jerusalem in AD 70, saying, *"For then shall be a great tribulation, such as was not since the beginning of the world to this time, no, nor ever shall be."* Those who had become Christians, whose names were written in the book of life, were "delivered" from spiritual death and from death in Jerusalem. See comments on Daniel 9:27.

And many of them that sleep in the dust of the earth shall awake, some to everlasting life, and some to shame and everlasting contempt. **12:2** The Jewish nation appeared to be dead without any hope when Antiochus IV killed over 80,000 Jews and desecrated the temple in Jerusalem. Their fathers also had been without hope as exiles in Babylon when the LORD spoke of their return to the land of Israel as a "resurrection" from their graves. [Ezekiel 37:11-14] So a resurrection may be used in a figurative sense to mean a revival and restoration. The Maccabees led by Judas came to life and drove the army of Antiochus out of Jerusalem and restored the worship of the LORD in his temple. They

---

[85] Charles F. Pfeiffer, *Between the Testaments* (Baker Book House, 1963)

will live forever in memory as long as Hanukkah is celebrated.

Those Jews that aided Antiochus will suffer shame and everlasting contempt. God spoke of Israel's future salvation in Christ as a resurrection. He said, *"O Israel, you have destroyed yourself; but in me is your help. . . I will ransom them from the power of the grave; I will redeem them from death."* [Hosea 13:9, 14] A person that believes in Christ has "passed from death to life." [John 5:24] We are raised from baptism to "walk in newness of life." [Romans 6:4]

The figurative use of words may serve as a type or shadow of the literal use. The Holy Spirit uses Hosea 13:14 to describe the literal resurrection of the dead at the end of time in 1 Corinthians 15:50-55. Although Daniel 12:2 had its first fulfillment in the figurative resurrection of the Maccabees, it also has its ultimate fulfillment in the literal resurrection of both the good and the evil when the Lord comes. [John 5:28-29]

And they that be wise shall shine as the brightness of the firmament; and they that turn many to righteousness as the stars forever and ever. **12:3** In Matthew 13:43, Jesus alludes to this verse and applies it to the righteous "in the kingdom of their Father" after the Judgment Day. Those faithful Jews that led others to righteousness are still greatly honored for saving their nation for the coming of Christ.

But you, O Daniel, shut up the words, and seal the book, even to the time of the end; many shall run to and fro, and knowledge shall be increased. **12:4** John Copeland makes these excellent comments on this verse. "Daniel was told to seal the prophecy until the time of the end, that is, until the time of its completion or fulfillment, not the end of time. Many people were to go to great lengths ('run to and fro') in an effort to understand the meaning of Daniel's prophecy, and knowledge will be increased. Daniel's prophecies could not be fully understood before they were fulfilled, but today, if we have the desire and are willing to study, we can understand them." [86]

Then I, Daniel, looked, and there before me stood two others, one on this bank of the river and one on the opposite bank. One of them said to the man clothed in linen, who was above the waters of the river, "How long will it be before these astonishing things are fulfilled?" **12:5-6** [NIV] "The man clothed in linen" was the angel that appeared to Daniel with the prophecy of the latter days of the Jews. [10:4, 5, 14] As this angel hovered above the Tigris River, Daniel saw two other angels, one on each side of the river. One of them wanted to know how long it would be before the fulfillment of this prophecy.

The angel clothed in linen raised both hands to heaven and ***swore by Him who lives forever, that it shall be for a time, times and a half a time.*** **12:7** [NKJV] It would be for three and a half years. Paul Butler says, "This can only have reference to the extraordinary terrors of the reign of Antiochus IV—not to some New Testament 'Antichrist' removed by at least some 2,000 years from those Old Testament saints for whom the revelation was given. Now it happens that from the time that Antiochus IV first removed the daily sacrifice from the Temple until Judas Maccabeus purified the Temple it was a little over three and a half years. So the angel dressed in linen answered that the time of extraordinary terror for the holy people will be, in round numbers, three and a half years." [87] When God's people seemed to be completely defeated, deliverance would come."

---

[86] John A. Copeland, *A Study of Daniel*, p. 63-64
[87] Paul T. Butler, *Daniel*, p. 455

Although I heard, I did not understand. Then I said, "My lord, what shall be the end of these things?" **12:8** Daniel still did not understand, and he asked for a more detailed explanation. The angel answered, *"Go your way, Daniel, for the words are closed up and sealed till the time of the end."* **12:9.** He was telling Daniel to get on with his life because the prophecy had been sealed, or reserved, until the time for its fulfillment near the end of the old covenant.

"Many shall be purified, and made white, and tried; but the wicked shall do wickedly, and none of the wicked shall understand, but the wise shall understand." **12:10** At that time, the wise would understand the prophecy of Daniel 10-12, and they would purify themselves by restoring the worship of the LORD after the forces of Antiochus had been driven from Jerusalem. The wise would "shine like the brightness of the heavens." [12:3, NIV] Daniel had been reading Jeremiah's prophecies that not only predicted the return from exile but also the replacement of the covenant of Moses with the new covenant of Christ.[88] From the days of the Maccabees, the faithful Jews were looking for their Messiah to come.[89] But the wicked would not understand and would continue in the pagan ways they had learned from the Greeks.

And from the time that the daily sacrifice shall be taken away, and the abomination that makes desolate set up, there shall be a thousand two hundred and ninety days. **12:11** The angel explains in more detail that the time would be 1,290 days from the desecration of the temple until its rededication to the Lord. John Copeland states, "There is no symbolic numbers in 1290 days; that was the literal time which elapsed between the

---

[88] Daniel 9:2, Jeremiah 29:10, Jeremiah 31:31-34, Hebrews 8:8-12
[89] Luke 2:25-38

elimination of the burnt offerings and their resumption. Epiphanes' decree to abolish the burnt offerings was issued on what would be, by our calendar, May 25, 168 BC. The burnt offerings were resumed on what would be, by our calendar, December 25, 165 BC, after the Maccabees had recaptured Jerusalem and had cleansed the temple of its abominations. That was 1290 days, a little over 3½ years." [90]

"Blessed is he who waits, and comes to the thousand three hundred and thirty-five days." **12:12** [NKJV] Paul Butler says, "Now add to the 1,290 days 45 more days, and one has 1,335 days, the time from the abomination that makes desolate until the time of Antiochus' death!" [91] These detailed predictions would be a source of encouragement and blessing to the faithful Jews during these distressful days.

"But you, go your way till the end; for you shall rest, and will arise to your inheritance at the end of those days." **12:13** [NKJV] Daniel is told not to worry because he would be at rest during this terrible time. He would be blessed by the coming of the Messiah at the end of these days.

The prophecies of Daniel are about events from the Babylonian exile to the days of the Romans, when the God of heaven would establish his eternal kingdom. [Daniel 2:44] The Most High rules!

---

[90] John A. Copeland, *A Study of Daniel*, p. 64
[91] Paul T. Butler, *Daniel*, p. 461

Review Questions on Lesson 13

1. The reign of _____ is summarized in Daniel 11:36-45.

2. What king called himself *"Theos"* (God) on his coins, and exalted himself above every god? [11:36]

   _____

3. The "indignation" or "wrath" in 11:36 refers to God's punishing the _____ because of transgressors among them in the second century BC.

4. Antiochus IV had no regard for _____, the god of his fathers, but he honored _____, claiming to be the incarnation of this Roman god.

5. Verses 40-43 summarize the _____ of Antiochus IV.

6. In 165 BC, Judas Maccabeus regained possession of the city of _____ and cleansed the _____.

7. Antiochus IV came to "his end" when he died in 164 BC by the hand of ____ _____.

8. The angel is explaining the future of the _____ in chapter twelve.

9. This is the same period as the _____ _____ that would be for the Jews and for Jerusalem in Daniel 9:24.

10. This time is from the Jews' return from _____ to the destruction of Jerusalem in AD _____.

11. After a difficult war against the Syrians, the Jews were able to gain their independence in May, _____ BC.

12. The Jews lost their freedom in 63 BC, when the _____ invaded their land under Pompey.

13. God would protect the Jews as a nation through troublesome times until his _____ was established in the first century AD.

14. Jesus said that Daniel 12:1 is describing the destruction of the city of _____ in the first century.

15. Daniel 12:2 predicted a _____ resurrection of the Maccabees, but it has its ultimate fulfillment in the _____ resurrection when the Lord comes again.

16. From the days of the Maccabees, the faithful Jews were looking for their _____ to come.

17. The 1,290 days in Daniel 12:11 were from the removal of the daily _____ to their restoration.

18. The 1,335 days in 12:12 were from the desecration of the _____ to the death of _____.

NOTES

Bibliography

Barnes, Albert, *Isaiah*. Barnes' Notes on the Old Testament
Grand Rapids, Michigan: Baker Book House, 1963 reprint.

Barnes, Albert, *Daniel*. Barnes' Notes on the Old Testament.

Bruce, F.F., *The Spreading Flame*. Grand Rapids, Michigan:
Wm. B. Eerdmans Publishing Company, 1961

Burns, Edward McNall, *Western Civilizations*, New York:
W. W. Norton & Company, Inc., Eighth Edition, 1973

Butler, Paul T., *Daniel*. Joplin, Missouri: College Press, 1982.

Coffman, James Burton, *Daniel*. Coffman's Bible Commentary.
Austin, Texas: Firm Foundation Publishing House.

Culver, Robert D., *Daniel*. The Wycliffe Bible Commentary.
Nashville, Tennessee: The Southwestern Company, 1962.

Copeland, John A., *A Study of Daniel*. Abilene, Texas:
Quality Publications, 1973

Farrar, F. W., *The Book of Daniel*. New York: Eaton & Mains,
Cincinnati: Jennings & Graham.

Hailey, Homer, *A Commentary on Isaiah*. Grand Rapids, Mich.:
Baker Book House, 1985. Reprint: Louisville, Kentucky:
Religious Supply, Inc., 1992.

Halley, Henry H., *Bible Handbook*. Chicago, Illinois: 1957.

Josephus, Flavius, *Antiquities*, translated by William Whiston.
Grand Rapids, Michigan: Kregel Publications, 1973.

Josephus, Flavious, *Wars of the Jews*. translated by W. Whiston.
Grand Rapids, Michigan: Kregel Publications, 1973

Keil & Delitzsch, *Commentary on the Old Testament*. Biblesoft

Maier, Paul L., *Eusebius—The Church History*. Grand Rapids:
Kregel Publications, 1999.

McGuiggan, Jim, **The Book of Daniel**. Lubbock, Texas:
Montex Publishing Company, 1978.

North, Stafford, *Studies in Daniel*. Oklahoma City, Oklahoma:
Oklahoma Christian University, 1990

Pfeiffer, Charles F., *Between the Testaments*. Grand Rapids:
Baker Book House, 1963

Peloubet, F. N., *Peloubet's Bible Dictionary*. Philadelphia:
The John C. Winston Company, 1947

Shackelford, Don, *Truth for Today Commentary, Isaiah*.
Searcy, Arkansas: Resource Publications, 2005

Suetonius, *Lives of the Twelve Caesars*. Internet

Thomson, J. E. H., *Daniel*, The Pulpit Commentary, Vol. 13.
Grand Rapids, Mich.: Wm. B. Eerdmans Publishing Co., 1962

Trench, Richard, *Notes on the Miracles*. Westwood, New Jersey:
Fleming H. Revell Company

Young, Edward J., *An Introduction to the Old Testament*.
Grand Rapids: Wm. B. Eerdmans Publishing Co., 1960